HIS HAND IN OUR LIVES

By
Gail Blanchard Huffman
Missionary to France

Copyright © 2017 by Gail Blanchard Huffman

All Rights Reserved

August, 2017

ISBN 978-0-9985452-0-2

All Scripture quotes are from the King James Bible unless verses are compared and then the source is identified.

No part of this work may be reproduced without the expressed consent of the publisher, except for brief quotes, whether by electronic, photocopying, recording, or information storage and retrieval systems.

Address All Inquiries To:

THE OLD PATHS PUBLICATIONS, Inc.
142 Gold Flume Way
Cleveland, Georgia, U.S.A.
Web: www.theoldpathspublications.com
E-mail: TOP@theoldpathspublications.com

DEDICATION

To my dear husband, Robert (Bob) Huffman, who followed his Lord, obeyed His call, and accomplished his task in spite of many hindrances and difficulties. Often he asked the Lord, "Why me? I don't have the aptitude or the qualifications to work with such a cultured and educated people!" And God aswered, "But you have perseverance, a burden for these people, and a servant's heart."

> *"Also I heard the voice of the Lord, saying, Whom shall I send, and who will go for us? Then said I, Here am I; send me. And he said, Go, and tell this people."* Isaiah 6; 8,9.

To our children and grandchildren, lest they forget.

To the people of France, some of whom have heard the message of Christ's love and sacrifice. To those who know not The Savior: May God send others so that all may hear!

> *"And we know that all things work together for good to them that love God, to them who are the called according to his purpose."* Ro 8:28 KJV

ACKNOWLEDGEMENTS

Sincere and heartfelt thanks to my eldest granddaughter Aloice, who typed three-fourths of the book as she bravely deciphered my handwriting.

Thanks also to Chantal who managed to type a readable version in spite of additions, retractions, and much rearranging.

Many thanks go to my publisher, H.D. (Doc) Williams and his wife Patricia, for their patience, understanding, and the superb help and guidance along the way.

I am very grateful to my son-in-law Sebastien who kept my computor running and took the photos for the cover; to my youngest grandson Odran, who seconded his dad when the computor decided to take a break; and to my youngest granddaughter Cenedra (Cissi) whose hands are featured on the front cover.

I shall not forget my dear friend Margaret, who not only encouraged me, but also designed the front cover.

To the One who inspired me to put His wonderful works in writing go praise and adoration for upholding me every day in spite of many discouragements. Thank you Lord!

FOREWORD

In reminiscing over years past, the thought comes to mind that God's Hand left its mark so many times in our life together. He answered countless prayers and directed us in many, many ways. Therefore, by putting them in print, I would like to share some of these incidents, first of all with my loving family and with my dearest friends and Christian brothers and sisters, and then with anyone else who may read these lines.

We all remember how certain events fell into place in our past which led us to a particular place, to a special job or profession, or to meet a special person. At times circumstances held more weight than our personal choices. I firmly believe that these circumstances were divinely sent to guide us to the path He has chosen for each of us. It is certain that in my life I can see how this came about so many times, as well as in our life together.

It is for this reason that I am penning these lines. To give credit to the One who has lovingly guided me all these years. He has never failed me when I called on Him, and even though many times I could not understand just where He was leading, I trusted Him and followed Him; and I have no regrets.

TABLE OF CONTENTS

DEDICATION 3
FOREWORD 5
TABLE OF CONTENTS 6
RESUME.. 7
CHAPTER ONE: WHERE HE LEADS….. 8
CHAPTER 2: "WHERE GOD GUIDES, GOD PROVIDES!" ... 18
CHAPTER 3: OUR WEDDING 25
CHAPTER 4: GOD'S CALL.. 37
CHAPTER 5: BEGINNING THE MINISTRY 51
CHAPTER 6: EVANGELISM.. 60
CHAPTER 7: WORKING WITH CHILDREN AND YOUTH.. 69
CHAPTER 8: THIS OLD HOUSE.. 88
CHAPTER 9: BURSTING AT THE SEAMS 100
CHAPTER 10: OUR OWN BUILDING 109
CHAPTER 11: THE HUFFMAN HOTEL.................................... 121
CHAPTER 12: THE LATER YEARS: BOB'S ILLNESS 134
CHAPTER 13: HIS LAST DAYS.. 150
CHAPTER 14: BOB HUFFMAN, A MAN OF CHARACTER!157
CHAPTER 15: THE HUFFMAN KIDS....................................... 164
CHAPTER 16: THREE WEDDINGS 211
CHAPTER 17: BOB'S YOUTHFUL YEARS............................. 227
CHAPTER 18: GAIL: GROWING UP.. 231
CHAPTER 19: WHY WE STAYED.. 249
CHAPTER 20: HIS HAND STILL GUIDES 257
ABOUT THE AUTHOR... 265

RESUMÉ

Discover the story of the Huffman family; how God brought them together, called them to serve, and accompanied them for over 40 years as they shared the love of Christ with their beloved French friends and neighbors. Every facet of ministry was explored; each level of society was touched.

With their French brothers and sisters beside them, they taught God's Word, held special meetings, including concerts and films followed by debates, and presented evangelistic messages. They distriibuted thousands of Gospel tracts, sponsored recorded telephone messages, and offered the precious gift of a New Testament to 28,000 homes in their town. Their children shared the ministry and labored beside their parents, inviting friends, helping with music and with meal preparation for the many friends who visited in the Huffman home.

In all their activities they saw the hand of the Lord guide them along the way, sometimes sown with obstacles which only God could help them overcome.

CHAPTER ONE: WHERE HE LEADS...

"He leadeth me beside the still waters." Psalm 23:2b

Pack My Bags

"Pack your bags and come" the registrar intoned over the phone 3 days before registration at the university began.

When my step-mother, Eloise, came into the living room that Tuesday morning, I shared the developments with her. My heart's desire was to go to a Christian college even though I had registered for courses at the University of South Florida and was scheduled to begin the following week. I explained, "I really feel this is what the Lord wants me to do! I have turned my life over to Him and my desire is to serve Him."

She stood there smoking a cigarette for an eternity as she thought things over. Finally, she replied, "Well, what do you need?" She knew that to go away to college, I would need certain items, so we began making plans: an alarm clock, a study lamp, a suitcase, as well as warmer clothes.

CHAPTER 1: WHERE HE LEADS

My Longing

During my last two years of High School, my longing to go to a Christian Bible School or university became more and more intense. However, my parents were opposed to my going away because of the cost and distance. They had offered to fix up the garage apartment, where my Gramps had lived there at home, and had purchased an older car for me to use commuting to USF. Therefore, this new development took my parents by surprise. Because I was the oldest, they had not had the experience of seeing one of their offspring leave the nest and it was not something I had planned to do behind their backs!

High School

My senior year of High School had been filled with tests, outings, friends, and plans for the future. I had ended the relationship with my boyfriend and he had left to join the military. At the end of the year, one of the most important events was in the planning of the Senior Prom! Even though I didn't have a date, I planned to go with girlfriends and had made a beautiful, long white evening gown of peau de soie with a large red bow in the back.

Carolyn, one of my good friends, was engaged to Danny and regretted that I didn't have a date. One spring evening in April, she and Danny went to the roller-skating rink where they renewed acquaintance with an old school friend who had just returned from doing duty in the Air Force. He was lamenting the fact that all the girls he knew before leaving were either married or engaged; not one single one was unattached! Carolyn asked him if he would be interested in going out with a friend of hers. He was willing to try, so Carolyn set the date for the four of us to go get a hamburger.

Blind Date

When Carolyn called me, I didn't know how to answer at first. I had never gone out on a blind date! But I had confidence in Carolyn, therefore I agreed to go. When we were introduced, I was impressed by his clean-cut good looks, his ready smile, his kindness, and his name, Bob Huffman. We enjoyed each others company from the start, and before they took me home that evening, Bob asked me to go to church with him the following Sunday.

Something On His Mind

While getting to know each other, we were encouraged to learn that we had a similar outlook on several subjects, one of them being our faith in God and the Bible. We continued attending church services together and as I studied the lessons, the Lord showed me my need to be baptized. Others were waiting to be baptized, among them being

CHAPTER 1: WHERE HE LEADS

Bob's mother, Helen. So, one July Sunday afternoon we were baptized, one by one, as a sign of the death, burial and resurrection of the Lord Jesus Christ. This step of obedience is an outward manifestation of our faith as well as a testimony to the unsaved world. The greatest privilege was to be called to serve the Lord!

Bob and I dated that spring and all summer after we met. We double-dated with Carol and Danny to the Senior Prom, and went out to the lake after the prom to talk and enjoy the summer evening. The next day Bob came over and brought a graduation present, a set of silverware. I was surprised, but it was a practical gift. Eloise said to me later, "He has something on his mind!" His aunt and uncle drove down from Ohio to visit his folks, and Bob took me to meet them, or rather, so they could meet me!

Because both of us were working weekdays, often we only saw each other on weekends. He lived across town from my house and it took a while for him to get home. One nice day we went to the beach, another to the lake, and one night after he took me home, he went to sleep at the wheel and ran off the road into a concrete bridge and totaled his car. I was thankful he wasn't hurt! The police said he was so relaxed he didn't even have whiplash! He was concerned about acquiring another vehicle, which seemed impossible since he hadn't finished paying for the Ford, and his insurance didn't give him enough to buy another one! The Lord had surprises for us and a few days later he came to pick me up in a 1946 model that his grandparents had given him. They were aging and didn't drive anymore. It was unusual to see a young fellow driving an ancient model such as that!

Will You Marry Me?

One day when Bob came by to get me, he told me his mother had a gold ring with a diamond set in that had been in the family for years. The band was damaged and bent so would I try it on to see if it fit? It was not my size so he measured my ring finger in order to have it repaired and sized. When it was ready he brought it and tried it on my finger. I looked at him and queried, "Aren't you going to ask me something?" "Will you marry me?" was his answer. "Yes, I would be proud and happy to be your wife. But first, before I go in the house wearing an engagement ring, you will need to ask my dad for permission since I am not yet 21." So he climbed out of the car to go talk to my parents who were in the back yard. He hem-hawed around, talking about everything except our future wedding. Finally, after more than an hour, here he came announcing, "He said all right!" So that evening we became officially engaged. To celebrate, the next day he brought an electric frying pan as an

CHAPTER 1: WHERE HE LEADS

engagement gift. Yes, he really did have something in mind!

We didn't talk about setting a date or anything pertaining to the future because I had told him, first I wanted to get more education. So we continued seeing each other, going to church together, and working in our respective jobs.

About a month later, on a Sunday morning after church, one of the girls in youth group came to tell us goodbye. She was leaving for a year of study at a Bible Institute in Chattanooga, Tennessee. Her parents were driving her to Tennessee Temple University.

The Desire

The deep desire of going to a Christian college re-surfaced in my spirit and I began asking her questions about Tennessee Temple. The more she explained, the more questions came to mind. To prepare to serve the Lord became a burning desire, and I couldn't stop asking questions. Barbara's parents invited Bob and me to their home for a quick lunch so that I could look through the catalog from the Bible college. As I looked and we talked, I became convinced that this was where I should be going. It was not just a personal desire, it was also the Lord who gave me this longing to study there. Barbara's parents sensed the intensity of this desire and offered to take me with them on Thursday.

Bob and I got in the car and went to a place where we could pray and talk. That evening after church services, we had prayer again after talking more about all the details of a possible departure. The next day was Labor Day – a holiday, therefore nothing could be done. It was a long 24 hours for me. Tuesday morning dawned bright and sunny. As soon as the offices opened at 8:30 A.M., I picked up the phone and asked about the possibility of registering for classes which began the following week. The Dean asked several questions about my salvation experience, Christian life, and high school grades. Then he asked for my pastor's phone number and said he would call me back after talking with him.

Pack Your Bags

I was sitting right next to the phone when it rang. The Dean's first words were, "Pack your bags and come!" I'll never forget them! He had as much faith in accepting me as I had in leaving my home, my fiancé, my family and my job, and setting out for the unknown! Deep down it felt so right, and I was more than excited about going; I was elated!

After I told my stepmother about this unexpected development, and she was able to think clearly, we began making preparations. With a large family there was rarely any extra money, so she got out her precious hoard of green stamp books to

CHAPTER 1: WHERE HE LEADS

use as collateral for what I would need, and left to make the purchases while I began packing. That afternoon when I went to work at the drugstore, I gave my notice, which was accepted without any problem since they knew I would be starting college anyway. The next day I got out the pattern and material I had purchased recently, cut out a dress and sewed it up, leaving the hem to do later by hand.

Before leaving, there was one bit of unfinished business that I needed to take care of. When I called Bob to inform him of being accepted at the Christian College, I told him I wanted to see him before leaving on Thursday. He came right after getting off work, so since the children were all home from school, we sat in the car to talk. I told him that I didn't think it would be right to hold him to an engagement if I was far away, and more important, I had no idea what the Lord wanted me to do during my studies and afterwards. With tears in my eyes I gave his ring back and said that he should date some of the nice girls at church as long as we weren't sure about the future; whether it held the possibility of us being together or separated. He was touched by my honesty and promised to call me sometimes on weekends. Thus we parted with heavy hearts.

Off to Tennessee

On Thursday morning, the Turner family came to pick me up, and I was off to Tennessee to begin college. I remember, as we neared Chattanooga, going through the tunnel in East Ridge, looking out over the city in the valley and thinking. "I wonder what the future holds for me in this place." Upon our arrival at the welcome desk, we were assigned to our dorm rooms and given a schedule for the first days before classes began, which included testing, orientation, and student revival meetings in the evenings.

Classes began the following Monday and my next preoccupation was; how will I pay my school bill? My savings would be gone in a couple of months and I had no scholarship. My parents couldn't help because there were six other children back home, of which I am the oldest. I needed to find part-time work!

The Influence of God's Words

A couple weeks later, as I was thinking about recent happenings, the thought came to mind, What am I doing here? I am studying at a Christian College, preparing to do what? Nearly all the students that I met had grown up in Christian homes and knew that the Lord had called them to be a preacher, a teacher, or perhaps a missionary. I picked up my Bible and continued reading in

CHAPTER 1: WHERE HE LEADS

Romans, where I was in my devotions, chapter 8. Verse 28 jumped out at me like a flashing light.

> *"And we know that all things work together for good to them that love God, to them who are the called according to his purpose."*

Yes, I loved the Lord and wanted to do His will. Was I called? Only He could have placed me here and worked out all the details! This verse was a great discovery for me; the answer to all my doubts and questions concerning the future! The Lord was in control and I could leave everything in His hands! He would lead, guide and provide!

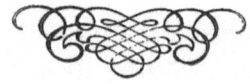

CHAPTER 2: "WHERE GOD GUIDES, GOD PROVIDES!"

"Therefore take no thought, saying, What shall we eat? or, What shall we drink? or, Wherewithal shall we be clothed?...for your heavenly Father knoweth that ye have need of all these things." Matthew 6:31,32b

Found a Job

Not too long after, I went by the personnel office where I checked regularly about a part-time job. That day there was a position for a team of students to run a line at McKee's Bakery in Collegedale, TN, working from 3 to 10 P.M., five evenings a week. A married student who had a car offered to take us and we would help with gas and other expenses. The pay was enough to cover my school bill, my tithe, and with enough left over for personal expenses. I accepted the position, thanking the Lord for His provision, not only for a job, but also for a way to get there and back.

So, we started out learning to run the line that made Little Debbie peanut butter wafers. First of all, one person mixed up the huge bowls of batter. Then he and his teammate measured out the correct amount of batter into the upright waffle

CHAPTER 2: WHERE GOD GUIDES, GOD PROVIDES

irons, which were heated to just the right temperature, and cooked the wafers. As they came off the waffle irons, they were sent down a short belt to cool off before being spread with the peanut butter filling. A cover was added and the two large filled wafers were sent by belt to a large roller, where they were compacted to just the right thickness.

The next step was to cut them into bars, which was done by a machine with thin wires running horizontally and vertically. These bars came off the cutting machine spaced out just right, and then sent into a tunnel where a spray covered them with hot chocolate syrup. The tunnel continued from one end of the line to the other and was refrigerated so that the bars came out cold and hard, ready to be wrapped individually and packed into boxes. That's where my friend, Sharon, and I worked. As the cookies came out of the tunnel, one of us would quickly slip them into slots on the wrapping machine, which was positioned at a 90 degree angle, so that each bar was wrapped in cellophane. At the end of that machine, one of us stood with a large table to the left and a huge pile of boxes with place for 12 bars in each. With the right hand we flipped the box open and set it down, slid four bars at a time into the box with three movements, then pushed the box away to the left where another person taped each box shut and filled a large carton with them.

In order to vary our tasks to avoid monotony of the production line, three or four of us would train for the different positions and switch off during the 8-hour stretch. The young man who ran and adjusted the machines was very production-minded, so as we trained he would slowly increase the speed of the machines. Thus, when we became agile at each task, we could work so fast that you could hardly see our hands. Soon we were going at top speed, and unless there were problems like pile-ups in one of the tunnels, we worked so well together and so fast that our team was at the top of the list of the production output!

At first, we enjoyed tasting the different bars and cakes, since the other lines made cream-filled oatmeal cookies or jelly rolls, but after a few weeks the odor took away our appetite for them, and to this day I cannot enjoy any of the products made there.

A Warm Coat

In October, the days began to be cooler; winter was coming! Being from Tampa, Florida, I had no winter coat, but the Lord knew all about it. Near the end of the month a package came from home for my birthday. To my surprise and delight, it contained, among other gifts, a soft warm beige

CHAPTER 2: WHERE GOD GUIDES, GOD PROVIDES

full-length winter coat. Before I even asked, the Lord had provided! My stepmother had exquisite taste, and also a flair for finding good quality clothes at unbelievably modest prices! I was now prepared for cold weather and thanked God for providing! Then I called home to thank my family.

The days were busy with classes, studying, working at the bakery, plus the church meetings. Once a week a special phone call came from Tampa. That young man to whom I had been engaged kept in touch even though he was dating other girls from church. He had found a better job at a print shop in Tampa, all the time seeking the Lord's will for the next step in his life. While working, he listened to Christian radio programs on the radio, and cried as he asked the Lord what He wanted him to do.

It became clear to him that he should join me in Chattanooga and begin preparing for some kind of service for the Lord. A few days before Thanksgiving he arrived in Chattanooga and found a room. We were so happy to see each other again, and he spent as much time as he could on campus so that we could be together. Once again he asked me to marry him. I still was not sure, so I asked him for a week to pray about it. I not only prayed; I agonized, asking the Lord what He wanted me to do. The problem was, I definitely felt that the Lord wanted me in full-time work for Him, and Bob didn't

HIS HAND IN OUR LIVES

know if he was called or not! After telling the Lord that my desire was to do His perfect will in my life, and that I would be willing to do anything or go anywhere, He began to show me that if I had confidence in Him, He would take care of Bob and make him into someone who could serve Him in a great way. That evening when I saw Bob, I told him 'yes', and shared how the Lord had given me complete peace about marrying him.

Bob's Starting Pay was $56.50!

We began making plans for Bob to begin classes the second semester in January, and for our wedding in June. A few days later as we were talking, Bob lamented, "After all that time in the barracks I really don't want to live in the dorm, not even for a semester!" Without thinking, I answered, "We could always get married after the first semester ends in January, and stay out one semester!" Immediately he said that was a good idea, and began going over the possibilities. The shock hit me as I realized that January was only two months away. How could we do it?

I began thinking about details. I called my stepmother to share the news with her, and she said she was willing to help get our wedding planned in just over one month. We called our pastor in Tampa and made arrangements with him. Then we began the paperwork at city hall, shopped

CHAPTER 2: WHERE GOD GUIDES, GOD PROVIDES

together for wedding bands, and got material for my dress. Bob continued looking for work and found a position in a print shop just two weeks before the wedding. His new boss even gave him a week off to get married! We could definitely see the Lord's hand in all of this, because since I was not yet 21, my dad would not give permission unless Bob had a job making at least $55 per week. Bob's starting pay was $56.50 per week. The Lord's hand was seen clearly in this answer to prayer! He doesn't make any mistakes! I asked for a week off from my job at the bakery, so the main events were lined up.

Things don't always line up exactly as one would wish, and even though we tried to take care of most of the details, my poor step-mother had her hands full. She had to find dresses for my two sisters that looked like the dress my maid of honor was to wear, among other things. It was a difficult task, but she came through with flying colors! Once, in all the hassle, she called me and said she felt like taking a shotgun to me for all the trouble I gave her. But her anger was temporary, and everything calmed down.

The last week in Chattanooga was exam week, so I had to concentrate on reviewing, plus working and taking care of last minute details. Since I didn't have a sewing machine, I found a seamstress who made my dress for a very reasonable price. Eloise had given me the ultimatum by saying that they couldn't afford a formal wedding. Therefore, my dress should be simple and street length, not floor length or with a train, and that it not be white because I would never wear it again. So, I found the palest pink and it looked nice with the blue dresses the girls wore.

After I finished my last exam on Friday, January 19, 1962, Bob and I set out for Tampa in his old car. We arrived late that evening, and the next morning the ladies from my parent's church had a surprise shower lined up. The ladies brought very nice and practical gifts, and I was overwhelmed at their kindness, especially since I didn't know any of them. Oh, the ignorance of youth! At age 17, I had never even been to a shower, and the only wedding I had ever attended was when my dad and Eloise were married 2 years earlier.

CHAPTER 3: OUR WEDDING

"And they shall be one flesh." Genesis: 2:24

The wedding was scheduled for Tuesday evening so that we could have a couple of days together before returning to Chattanooga. It took a lot of organization at home in order to get six other children fed and dressed for a wedding. Eloise was so good at organizing that everything went very smoothly. I tried to stay calm because she didn't need an excited or teary bride to deal with, too!

No Photos

When Bob arrived at the church, he took the last few snaps on the film in his camera, then put in a new role of film and asked his uncle to take pictures of the family and the ceremony. Somehow, the gears stripped the film and it didn't turn, leaving us with no photos. The Lord always has surprises for us, and when the pastor's wife learned about this, she had doubles made of the snapshots she had taken. We were very thankful and relieved to have a few nice photos, and had one enlarged to frame.

Before the ceremony began, the pastor took Bob and his best man into the little room behind the pulpit to give last minute instructions. He looked at Bob and said, "If you change your mind, it's not too late! I'll go out and tell everyone the wedding has been called off." I'm so glad he loved me enough to commit himself for life.

My maid of honor, Carolyn Mallory, was the friend who had introduced us just after Bob got out of the Air Force. My bridesmaid was my sister Carol, four years younger than I, and my flower girl was my little step-sister, Alice. The best man was Charles Briggs, Bob's buddy from high school who had witnessed to him and was overjoyed to learn that he had accepted Christ while in the Air Force. Charles' brother Danny, who was Carolyn Mallory's fiancé, was the groomsman. He had also been instrumental in introducing us.

The Ceremony

When the music began, I started down the aisle holding my dad's arm. Being the oldest, I was the first one he had to give away. Halfway down the aisle he almost tripped and I had to steady him so he wouldn't lose his balance. I realized he was more nervous than I was, but he was able to sit down a few minutes later and relax. One of the ladies was playing the Wedding March, followed by the interpretation by one of the young ladies that was in youth group of a song we liked entitled, "God Gave You to Me," written and put to music by

CHAPTER 3: OUR WEDDING

Charles Weigle. We repeated our vows and then kneeled and began our married life together with a prayer of benediction.

Our Wedding Day, January 23, 1962

Surprises

After the ceremony, we lined up with the family to greet our guests with the intention of leaving right after we changed clothes. The pastor took the microphone and announced, "The ladies of the church invite you to stay for a reception in the Fellowship Hall." A surprise reception! Unbelievable! As we entered the room, we saw a beautiful wedding cake surrounded by lovely flowers and decorations, and a table piled high with gifts. Our dear friends at church knew we couldn't afford such extras, so they planned it all without breathing a word. We spent an enjoyable evening with our families and friends from the Northgate Baptist Church where we were members.

As we prepared to leave, I went into a classroom to change into my going-away outfit: a turquoise wool suit that I had made while in high school, on which I had changed the collar and buttons from imitation leopard to white rabbit's fur for the occasion. Bob had rented a room on the beach and we were looking forward to relaxing and beginning our married life together. Our Sunday school teacher, Helen Elliot, who was helping me change, slipped around behind me and began putting rice in my undies. It was so uncomfortable, especially in the girdle I had on to look firm in my straight skirt.

CHAPTER 3: OUR WEDDING

In the meantime, Bob's parents had gotten into our well-decorated car while waiting for us to arrive. Someone gave us the keys to their car, so when our car left with everyone honking behind them, we got in the line and honked too! After a while we all stopped and switched cars, and we drove over to Clearwater Beach where we spent our one-night honeymoon. Unfortunately, because of so much activity, plus accumulated fatigue, I began running a fever. The next morning Bob took me to his doctor who gave me an injection before we started our drive back to Chattanooga. Both of us had to be back to work at the end of the week and needed to be in shape.

Picture Perfect

A couple of weeks earlier we had rented a furnished three-room apartment on Bailey Avenue, so upon arriving we unpacked our gifts and took in the couple pieces of furniture my folks had given us. My new husband had an interesting surprise waiting for me; 12 white shirts that had to be starched, dampened and ironed. He had saved them instead of sending them out since he now had a wife to take care of them. The next day I ironed them and hung them in our one and only closet, and when he came home he checked them and asked me to button the top button on each shirt so the collar would stand up straight! That was my initiation to the ways of a perfectionist.

HIS HAND IN OUR LIVES

During our first months of marriage, we adjusted well to married life, each enjoying our new "roommate." I invited the girls from my dorm for dinner one evening, and they were surprised that I knew how to cook! I continued working evenings at the bakery and Bob worked days at the print shop. When summer classes began, Bob quit his job and looked for something part-time. His boss liked his work, so offered him a raise and other benefits if he would stay. Bob said to himself, *"Get thee behind me, Satan"* and began classes.

Living on Less

We had found a less expensive apartment and moved before that summer. Our new landlady, Mrs. Jennings, was a widow who had brought up seven children, and a dedicated Christian who was a member of Woodland Park Baptist Church. She treated us like part of the family, and would bring us big bowls of beef stew or some other tasty dish saying, "Gail, honey, I made too much again and I get tired of eating the same thing every day. Would you like to finish this? I can't seem to cook for one person after cooking for my large family!" God provided for each and every meal, plus other expenses. While Bob looked for part-time work, we lived on $30 a week, which is what I made as a cashier in a large department store. We were just barely getting by, but told no one except the Lord. We continued to give our tithe and in the back of

CHAPTER 3: OUR WEDDING

Bob's Bible, we started a list of answers to prayer. In searching for a part-time job, Bob went to the unemployment agency downtown, and the only thing they had to offer him was a position going door-to-door selling waterless cookware. This was definitely not suited to his personality, but he tried it. In order to practice, he tried the "speech" on me, then on Mrs. Jennings. He soon learned that the names and addresses of families that he was to contact had been visited by someone previously. He returned the pans and went back to looking for a more suitable position.

Right up His Alley

After several more weeks of searching, he found an opening at a pharmacy that delivered many of their prescriptions, so he began driving the "Pill Wagon." This job fit like a glove, not only because he enjoyed driving, but also because they adapted his hours to his schedule at Bible College.

It was about this time that we began working at one of the chapels or "church plants" in the outskirts of Dalton, GA. We drove down early each Sunday morning to help with Sunday school and morning service, took our lunch and spent the day, holding evening services as well. This experience helped us learn how to teach children, lead singing, organize the services, as well as understanding

HIS HAND IN OUR LIVES

church government, and how to deal with spiritual problems.

That fall, Bob signed up for classes and I continued working as a cashier in a large store called Jubilee City, where I had found part-time work in the spring. I ended my time at McKee's Bakery because the sharp corners on the chocolate covered wafers cut my hands. I did not sign up for classes as planned because we found out in August that our first child was on the way, due in April, and my morning sickness was quite severe. Instead of gaining weight, I lost weight and no one could tell I was expecting! One evening at work when we were on break, we gathered in the ladies' room and my friend Sharon, who was expecting in April too, noticed I had on a maternity top for the first time. She pulled it up and burst out laughing at my more than flat tummy! I didn't "show" until I was more than 6 months along! This didn't prevent the baby from weighing almost 9 pounds! She didn't suffer from my discomfort.

Provisions

I continued to work as a cashier until after Christmas when I was laid off. In order to make ends meet, I began sewing for friends and students, and I prepared meals for a fellow who lived alone. The $7.00 a week that he gave us allowed us to buy groceries for the three of us. The

CHAPTER 3: OUR WEDDING

Lord always provided, for we never missed a meal and always gave the tithe of our income.

Eloise sent her maternity clothes early on, and later she sent the baby clothes she had saved after my little brother, Ralphie, was born. She also gave us the crib and stroller so we had the basics. I never wondered how we would manage. To me it was evident that the Lord would provide. Before we even asked the Lord for a washer, Bob's parents gave us the money to purchase one. With diapers to wash every day, it was well-appreciated.

Lauri Luann Huffman was born on April 18, two days after her due date. She weighed 8 lbs and 15 ounces and was 52 cm long. She was a big girl for being the first one. She resembled her dad's baby pictures and had blond fuzz and dark blue eyes. She was such a happy baby, always smiling and was content and sociable. She gained weight steadily and filled out early. When she was three months I took her to Florida so our families could become acquainted with her. Bob's mother especially enjoyed her since she had always wanted a girl.

Being a mother was especially rewarding for me, since my teenage years had been particularly difficult. Having a little one to care for, to talk to, and who needed me, gave me much satisfaction and made me feel worthwhile.

On Again, Off Again

In the fall, Bob returned to the Bible Institute and I stayed home with Lauri since I had already completed my first semester the previous year. In order to help out financially, I continued sewing for the girls at the college and worked evenings at the store where they had put me back on the payroll. Then, right after Christmas, I was laid off again, and we depended on the Lord to provide until we could find adequate work. God continued to provide in different ways and it was always exciting to see just how!

The following summer Bob found a much better paying job at Southeastern Wire Cloth in Chattanooga on the evening shift from 3 P.M. to midnight. Our two rooms became more and more crowded as Lauri grew and needed accessories. We prayed about what to do, and decided to purchase a house trailor and move to East Ridge. However, the payments, in addition to paying rent for the lot, proved to be too expensive since we were also paying our school bill. We ended up selling the trailor and moving into a rented apartment in Brainerd.

During our years in Bible college, we were certain that we were in the Lord's will but didn't know as yet just where the Lord wanted us in the future. Bob felt inadequate, saying that he couldn't

CHAPTER 3: OUR WEDDING

be a pastor because he couldn't preach, nor a song leader because he couldn't sing, nor a teacher because his grades weren't top. We began praying that the Lord would show us what He would have us prepare for and where.

Working full-time made it difficult for Bob to study as he desired, and his grades suffered. At the end of his second year he transferred to Bible Institute in order to bring his grades up. He decided to finish Bible School, and in 1967 he received his Bachelor of Bible diploma. His mother was so happy and proud, for he was the first one in the Huffman family to receive anything higher than a high school diploma. She and Tang drove up from Tampa to be there for the graduation.

They took advantage of the time in Chattanooga to spend time with their new granddaughter, for the Lord had blessed our family with a second daughter born four years after Lauri. When she was five months old I returned to classes and was able to finish my fourth year and receive my B.A. with a major in English in June of 1968, a year after Bob finished. For a time, he thought he was through with his studies, but since I had only one year left, he signed up for the fourth year of Bible School and only lacked 2 years of Greek to receive his Graduate of theology degree.

Bob receives his diploma, June 1967

CHAPTER 4: GOD'S CALL

"Then said I, Here am I; send me." Isaiah 6:8b

Searching For His Will

Every year in November the church where the students attended had a missionary conference and invited missionaries and representatives from many different countries. We always invited one of the missionaries to share a meal in our home, thus giving us the opportunity to ask questions. Each year we noticed that very few missions were reaching the countries of Europe. While Bob was stationed in Libya, North Africa, he was able to get free hops to visit several European countries, as well as to attend a couple of Christian conferences. Even back then the lack of outreach in Europe was obvious; a fact that turned our thoughts and hearts toward this need.

During one of the missionary conferences someone recommended the book LET EUROPE HEAR by Bob Evans. It focused our attention on the lack of Baptist and Evangelical churches in Europe where one could hear the Gospel and receive Christ. One afternoon the question of our future was especially on our minds, so we had a special time of prayer and told the Lord that we would go where He called us. We considered the different countries, and France kept coming to our minds. This seemed logical because I had studied French for two years and Bob for six months. It seemed the Lord was narrowing down the choice.

God calls us to France

In November 1967, we made application to Baptist International Missions as candidates to go to France; the first couple to go to there with BIMI. After acceptance, we began sending letters to churches that were mission-minded, sharing our burden to reach the French people for Christ. The first church that asked us to come was in Olney, Il

CHAPTER 4: GOD'S CALL

so we drove up to present the spiritual needs of France. We had bought some slides and borrowed others for a presentation, and had cards printed with a family photo, our address, and a resume of our desire to serve in France. More invitations began coming in, so in June after graduation we began traveling full-time, trusting the Lord for finances after Bob resigned from his position at work. We also gave up our apartment, packed our belongings in trunks and barrels, and stored them at the mission motel, where there were cabins for the missionaries to stay in while they were traveling on deputation or furlough.

Our travels took us from the Chattanooga area to Georgia, Alabama, Florida, then north to North Carolina, Virginia, West Virginia, Maryland, New York, Massachusetts, Vermont, then out west to Indiana, Missouri and Texas. Our vehicle was a small Toyota, one of the first sold in Chattanooga, and we put many miles on it! Since space was limited, we only took three traveling outfits and two Sunday outfits, and we washed twice a week so dirty clothes didn't accumulate. In most homes where we stayed, folks were kind enough to ask if we needed clothes washed, and other days we found a Laundromat. The people in the churches we spoke in were open and understanding, and very generous in sharing their homes and hearts with us. We made acquaintance with many wonderful people. Many have remained our friends over the years and still keep in touch.

By January

By January of 1969 we felt we were ready to leave, but the Lord kept us there until March, knowing we would need more monthly support than we had. We began looking for tickets, sold our car a month after making the last payment, added a few more belongings to our barrels and had them shipped. Ferrell and Barbara Kearney wrote and asked us to arrange for a stopover in Reykjavik, Iceland to spend a few days with them. They had been there for two years without having contact with other Christians and needed the fellowship. We enjoyed getting to know them and their two boys, and were amazed at how clean the capitol city of Reykjavik was! It was due to the fact that homes and buildings are heated with water from the hot springs. Dogs are not allowed in town so even the streets were extra clean! It was interesting to discover that being so close to the North Pole the nights were very short in March and everyone closed their shutters to keep out the sunlight and be able to sleep.

Three days later upon arriving in France at the Le Bourget airport north of Paris, George and Vera Palmer so graciously welcomed us to France and took us to the Aldin's home for dinner that

CHAPTER 4: GOD'S CALL

evening. We had been in touch with the Palmers by mail and they had arranged for us to rent an apartment near Paris while we began language studies. We asked if we could wash our hands before dinner, and discovered the bidet, which we had heard about; thus, our apprenticeship in becoming French had begun. We spent the next few days at the Palmers' high-rise apartment complex until we could get settled in our own apartment.

New Vocabulary

As we began to learn the ropes, we had to open a bank account, register for language school, have the water and electricity turned on in our apartment, make arrangements for our older daughter to go to school, and buy some groceries – all with the help of brother Palmer who spoke excellent French. Having studied 2 years of French in college, I was able to read enough French to buy groceries. However, speaking was another matter at first. There was a tiny grocery downstairs in our building, but it was not self-service and the owner didn't speak a word of English. The first time I went in was to buy some grape juice among other things and since I had started language school a few days before and thought I knew the right word, I ventured to ask him for some grape juice. "Jus de raison, jus de raison, non, I don't have any today," was his answer. "Mais du jus de raisin, si vous en voulez." Without realizing it, I had asked for reason juice instead of grape juice! I never forgot the difference, and paid more attention to just how I was pronouncing my newly learned French vocabulary. After that I looked around the neighborhood and found a larger store where I could pick and choose except for the butcher, where I had to order, but we got by and never went hungry.

What were our first impressions of France? One of my impressions was wall-to-wall people! I just couldn't get over the crowds when we went to Paris or its suburbs! Everything was so small compared to the US, all except the huge semi trucks! They are just as colossal!

As soon as we got settled, we began language studies in Paris. Bob would leave early for the morning class, then hurry home on the metro and train so I could leave for the afternoon class. I would warm up his lunch, then leave immediately to drop Lauri off at her school, and then catch the train for the Alliance Française. In this way one of us was always home with Licia –two years old- as well as be available to get Lauri after school. On pretty days, Bob would take the girls to the park since we had no yard, and I would go there from the train station. Often I made pancakes, so the girls had snack time called a "goûter" when we put sugar or jelly in the pancakes and rolled them up like crêpes.

CHAPTER 4: GOD'S CALL

On Sunday afternoons, we often took a walk (no car yet) and enjoyed becoming familiar with the neighborhood. Usually we ended up at the bakery and ordered the best-looking, richest French pastry we could find. Bob called it "culture shock" but it was really because we had a sweet tooth and wanted to taste every pastry in the window! And no, that didn't cause us to gain weight because we walked several kilometers a day going to the train station and into Paris for language studies and so on.

Our Girls Learn French

We began making acquaintance with some of the neighbors and since our street was a dead-end street, the children all played together at the end where there was rarely any traffic. They enjoyed roller-skating and playing ball, and began to pick up on French everyday expressions. One day when Bob had left with Lauri, I was cleaning the breakfast dishes and encouraged Licia to finish her hot chocolate. She didn't want to drink the rest and when I asked her why, she answered, "Because it's dirty in the bottom!" Another time after eating breakfast her tummy growled loudly, so teasingly I asked her "Your tummy is talking; what did it say?" Her answer "I don't know; it's speaking in French."

Lauri officially began the first grade in September at age 6½.

After 2 months of classes the previous spring, plus the 6½ weeks summer program, she spoke French quite fluently and was learning to read. Every evening one of us would sit down with her to review the lessons of the day, and going over the pronunciation of the vowels, vowel combinations, and consonants helped Bob and me, as well!

Progress in learning French seemed slow to us and our biggest need was to practice speaking, so in talking with Brother Palmer, he told us about a Christian lady who would help us with conversation and correct our phrasing and grammar. Thus, we met Mademoiselle Arion, a lovely white-haired lady who had never married and was retired from teaching. She was very patient with us, even when we made the same mistakes over and over. When Bob began writing out his messages, she corrected them and she helped us both greatly with Biblical language. The school year finished up at the end of June, but we continued our classes through July. We enrolled Lauri in the summer program so she could continue making progress in French. We wanted her to have a good grasp of language before learning to read.

Bob learned of a Christian camp in the Alps where he could go and not only help out, but also practice his French. So he signed up, bought a back-pack and hiking boots, and rode down with some other men for two weeks of total immersion.

CHAPTER 4: GOD'S CALL

They left the first day of August and at least half of the population of France was on the road leaving for their sacred one-month vacation. The traffic was so heavy that they just crawled along and they saw several accidents, including a car with its roof-top creased by a boat from behind when it stopped suddenly. We decided that we would try to avoid leaving on weekends or first of the month and later on we always started our camps or vacation on a week day.

While their dad was away, the girls and I did some special things, and I tried to rest a lot because I learned that our third child was on the way. In September, I modified my schedule in language school and did most of my work by correspondence, going to Paris only once a week for testing. I continued with Melle Arion, however, because she lived nearby.

In addition to classes at the Alliance Française, Bob enrolled in the civilization course at the Sorbonne. He learned much about the culture and history of France, and visited many monuments in Paris. In spite of the extra courses, he still had difficulties with spelling and grammar, but he persisted and even though he made a few mistakes here and there, his vocabulary was vast and he became proficient in French.

Wheels

As my pregnancy advanced, Bob began praying about purchasing a car. He did not want to get caught with his wife in labor during the night and no way to get to the hospital! He found a slightly used Toyota for a reasonable price which was just the right size for five, and became its owner. Then he went to the prefecture (county seat) to have his driver's license translated.

That fall our landlord, who was a pastor at a church in Evreux, asked Bob if he would be willing to fill in for him so he could have a much-needed vacation. He wrote out his messages and had Melle Arion correct them, then preached them over at the house. Every Sunday morning we left very early to drive the two hours, and became acquainted with the church family there. They were very gracious, and each week for four weeks invited our little family for the midday meal. It was a good experience and made us long to begin a ministry for our Lord, for all around we could see the need for good Bible-believing churches, which are still few and far between.

After a long winter, our son, Lance Timothy, was born on March 10, weighing 8 pounds 14 ounces. The day after his birth he developed a high fever and was transferred to a specialized hospital for 10 days. I left the hospital empty-armed. It was

CHAPTER 4: GOD'S CALL

a terrible feeling, and when I got to the car Licia was laughing with joy at seeing me, and Lauri was crying because the baby was not with me. I didn't know whether to laugh or cry. It was a very difficult time and we turned to the Lord and His promises for comfort. Bob drove to the other hospital in Paris so we could see how Lance was doing, and I found that almost 9 pound baby, had been put in a glass cradle for premature babies, which he filled up completely and could hardly move. When his health improved we took him home, but they never found out why he ran such a high fever. At the age of 4 months we took him back to the hospital for tests and everything checked out completely normal, for which we were praising the Lord!

The girls were enchanted with their baby brother, who was a calm, content baby. That summer, when he was 6½ months, we drove to the French Alps, to the camp where Bob had gone the previous summer, and stayed in lovely wooden chalet for a fortnight. It was a relaxing vacation which allowed us to test our conversational French when we went to the dining hall to enjoy a French meal with the campers. When both girls broke out with 3-day measles we isolated them and took their meals to the chalet, but were able to take walks on the beautiful mountainside.

In the fall, Licia was able to begin going to kindergarten. As long as a child was potty-trained

HIS HAND IN OUR LIVES

and age 3, they could begin going to "la classe des petits" and can go for three years until they are required to begin first grade at age 6. She still didn't speak much French but understood quite a bit. The first day we explained to her teacher, who was a Christian in the Brethren group, that she might not understand or participate because of the language barrier, and we kept in touch with her. By Christmas, she told us that Licia could speak and understand French as well as the other children her age! We were delighted that she had adapted so quickly! Oh, to learn French as rapidly!

In the spring of 1970, the missionaries with BIMI thought it would be a good time to have a European mini-conference, since the director was coming to visit the Paris area. Bob was nominated to find a place for us to spend a few days all together, and to assure transportation for each family, whether they arrived by plane, rail or highway. The Kearney's from England crossed the channel with their two boys; the Pauleys and their son, who were in France studying French before going to the Congo, joined us; the West's from Spain drove up with their three children, and a few other families studying in Paris were invited. We stayed at a conference center north of Paris called Saint Prix, and spent 3 days enjoying the fellowship, hearing messages, and singing in English. It was particularly refreshing after more

CHAPTER 4: GOD'S CALL

than a year of total immersion in the French language.

New Families

Two months later, in May of that same year, the Abbett family was scheduled to arrive to settle in and begin language studies. They felt called of the Lord to serve in France, so we were especially glad to have them arrive. A few days before their landing, Bob felt impressed to acquire a luggage rack for our Toyota, remembering how much space suitcases can take. Their two children were small, but so was the car! When he arrived at the airport on the appointed day, there were not one, but two families!!!– the Abbetts plus the Skeltons and their one-month old baby boy. Were we ever surprised! Arnold Skelton had tried to call us to let us know they would be coming, but since he didn't have our number, he got the wrong Huffman's. So in our small apartment, each family had a room. Praise the Lord we had purchased a sofa that pulled out and made a bed in the living room. There was a double bed in the girls' room for one of the families, and for the children we arranged palettes. For the baby, we brought the top part of the English-style carriage upstairs, so everyone was comfortable. We enjoyed being together and laughed a lot as we got to know each other. The Abbetts soon found an apartment in a neighboring town, and the Skelton's about a week later. Both couples began language training as soon as they got settled. It was nice to have colleagues with whom we could fellowship while our children enjoyed having new playmates.

As we made progress in French conversation, our desire to share Christ's love with friends and neighbors increased. We had been in touch with the workers at Child Evangelism Fellowship whose French office was right there in Colombes. Therefore, we asked them to come once a week to our apartment and begin a Bible Club. A few of the neighbor children attended and after a few weeks Bob and I began to prepare the songs and stories ourselves and share them with the children. We were thankful when the children corrected our mistakes; we tried to remember and not make the same ones again. It was humbling, but an efficient way to improve conversational French! We also began an English conversation course to reach youth and adults. One young lady professed Christ, but soon moved away and we lost touch with her. A teenage girl also shared with us of her new-found faith in Christ, but she worked in the open market on Sunday, then went away to begin her studies. We were thankful for these two, and look forward to renewing acquaintance one day in heaven.

CHAPTER 5: BEGINNING THE MINISTRY

"...grant unto thy servants, that with all boldness they may speak thy word." Acts 4:29b

As we became more proficient in French, our desire to begin a work in the place God had called us became more pronounced. Across the Seine River from Colombes was a town called Argenteuil with a population of nearly 100,000 and only one evangelical group. On the northern edge of town, a whole new "city" was under construction, with not only 20-25 large apartment buildings, but also a sporting complex, several schools, a shopping center with underground parking, and even a new train station! It was large enough for the projected 20,000 people to live comfortably, and all new! We checked to see if there would be a church, but none was planned, so we began to pray about moving there, not only to begin a work, but also to have more room for our growing family. That fall we signed to rent a 5-room apartment on the 4th floor of a 20-floor high rise. We could not move in until the end of December, but found out that the floors, which were wooden parquet, were unfinished. Bob rented a large electric sander and sanded them

HIS HAND IN OUR LIVES

smooth a few days before we moved in. Our plan was to varnish them but it would have taken too long to dry before we had to be out of our old apartment, so we gave them a thick coat of special wax and they looked great!

We moved at the end of December and were getting settled when Licia, age 4, began running a high fever and broke out with a bright pink rash. We asked neighbors about a doctor and got a rendezvous. He diagnosed her as having scarlet fever, prescribed medication, and told us how to care for her. The fever was so high that I put her bed next to mine and got up every hour all night to cool her off a bit and give her a drink. After two weeks she started getting better, but then broke out with another rash but had less fever. Back to the doctor we went, who said she had the measles which she contracted because her immune system was weakened. He prescribed gamma globulin injections to build up her resistance. After 4 weeks of illness she was pale and thin, but feeling better. We thanked the Lord for good medical care in France and for restoring her health!

As we discovered our new neighborhood, we again began English classes to reach the teens especially. Since our arrival in France we had been attending the evangelical church in Petit Colombes. The pastor, Joseph Danet, encouraged us to begin meetings in Argenteuil, putting us in contact with a

CHAPTER 5: BEGINNING THE MINISTRY

family in our apartment complex who was in agreement to coming for Bible studies and eventually, Sunday Services. The family included six girls, so what could we do but begin a Bible Club? Other children began to come as the girls invited them, and many children came and heard the Gospel one time. Most of them were of Catholic families and some went to catechism, but many had other activities at that time of day, or did not come back because their parents were not comfortable with the unknown. Protestants are few and far between and the French have a very limited understanding of their beliefs. One mother told her daughter that if she came to the Bible Club she would turn black! (Meaning like a nun dressed in black)

The Bible Club grew in spite of this, so we began to look around for a meeting place larger than our living room. Bob learned that there was a room available for public meetings in a nearby apartment building, so went to talk to the woman in charge. She gave us temporary permission to use it on Wednesday afternoon when the children had no school, but informed us that to use it regularly we needed to write for permission from the mayor's office. At this time the mayor and his "team" were communist. As soon as they received our request, they called the woman in charge and said that under no circumstances were we to have permission to use that room! We understood that we could not depend on public officials to be behind our efforts to share the Gospel, therefore we began praying for the Lord to show us another path to take. We continued meetings in our living room, adding Sunday morning services to the Bible Club, English classes and Bible study.

On Sunday morning when people came, we began Sunday school for the children in the girls' bedroom. The father of the six girls went in afterwards to get his youngest and came out chucking. He showed me the doll's bed with two dolls in it, one white and one black, and said,"No racist's here! Even the dolls integrate!"

We had been living in the apartment complex for over a year when our guardian came by and informed us that we were not allowed to invite the public to our apartment because it increased the use of the elevator and lighting in the halls and the cost was divided among the residents. Bob began looking around for a house where we could have the liberty to meet, and our Christians prayed with us for a room not far from the apartment complex. Soon after, he found a place about 6-8 blocks away with adequate space for our family on the main floor, plus a full basement with garage to be used as a chapel, a large room for the children's and youth work, a smaller room for an office, and a large back yard. With praise for his answer to

CHAPTER 5: BEGINNING THE MINISTRY

prayer, we signed the papers to rent the house at 50, rue du Coq (Rooster Road). On the day we moved, several men of our group began transforming the garage while the others helped get our furniture and belongings in the right places. It was quite a production! God gave strength and blessings, and the very next day we held our first Sunday morning services in the newly transformed chapel!

Now with more room, we were able to invite more children for the Bible Club, and soon Bob was bringing 2-3 VW busloads from our former neighborhood. Many of these children were Algerian, Moroccan or Tunisian with an Islamic background. They enjoyed coming and were a very enthusiastic group! Then one Wednesday, about 2-3 months later, none of these children came. We found out that someone had gone through the apartment buildings and told the parents not to allow them to come anymore; that it was not for them, and to fill the void they began a course in reading and writing Arabic for children. A few of them had made professions of faith so we tried to stay in touch with them and encourage them as best we could.

By that time the children in our new neighborhood were coming so attendance went back up. The English class was turned into a youth group that came on Saturday and many more youth were reached when their friends invited them to come and play ping-pong. Game time was followed by a meditation and question time, and often we added special meetings with a film, a Christian choir, or an outing. By these and other means the Gospel was shared and a few came just out of curiosity to hear what the Bible teaches.

Two young hippies were invited to the Bible Study by Monsieur Landou, father of the six girls. They asked questions constantly and Bob took time to explain God's plan of salvation to each of them individually. Both of them professed their faith in Christ, and after a few weeks they asked to be baptized. Where to go? We didn't even have a bathtub and there were no lakes in the area, only the Seine River which was entirely too deep and polluted as well. Bob began looking farther away from towns and congested areas, and found an abandoned quarry that had filled with water over time. We announced the baptism to those who attended and all drove out to have a lakeside meeting where Bob baptized Jean-Yves and Jacques. It was a special blessing to see, and the kingdom of heaven increased by two souls "The people which sat in darkness saw great light..." When they first began coming to the Bible Study they arrived dressed in jogging suits and their hair was shoulder-length. As they read and studied their Bibles on their own, they began to come in dress

CHAPTER 5: BEGINNING THE MINISTRY

shirts and dress pants and one after the other had their hair cut. The Lord had shown them without anyone bringing up the subject.

The First Baptism

Living in an apartment had limited our ministry, but there were ways of getting the Word out to the people. One method was by putting posters with a message on public signboards. The men would go out in the evenings after work and, with buckets of well-paper paste, glue the posters on the boards that were installed for the public to use, one in every neighborhood. The next day many of them were already covered up. We also used "sandwich men," that is Christians who walked around with panels on the front and back, held together on their shoulders, announcing a special meeting and sharing a message or verse from the Bible. Very few folks came because of publicity out of fear of the unknown, but as the Christians studied their Bibles, they began inviting family members, friends, neighbors, and colleagues. Our group grew to about 35 on Sunday mornings and 10-12 on Wednesday evenings.

One family became very special to us after they had been coming for several weeks. The oldest daughter of the eleven children had written a letter to us when she learned about our meetings, saying that she had recently found the Lord and was praying for the rest of the family. Her letter included a list of her ten brothers and sisters with explanations concerning their work and spiritual inclination. She was very concerned about them all coming to know Christ. After a visit and an invitation from Bob, the mother and two of the daughters began coming to services. One by one the three of them came to the Savior and were baptized, this time in a neighboring church that loaned us their facilities. Another daughter had not only deep-seated psychological problems, but was on drugs as well. After visiting her several times, it seemed there was no progress or change, so Bob sat down on the floor in front of her door and said he would not leave until she promised to attend services. She was present for the following Sunday

CHAPTER 5: BEGINNING THE MINISTRY

services, heard the Gospel again, and later on after getting help with her drug problem, she found Christ and new life in Him. We were overjoyed, as was her family! One of her sisters had committed suicide so the change in her was an enormous relief, especially to her mother! This family was faithful to the Lord and to the church for about 35 years until the mother went to her heavenly home at age 95. The family home was sold and the others moved away and found other church-homes.

Mother's Day in our first chapel

CHAPTER 6: EVANGELISM

"The Lord gave the word: great was the company of those that published it." Psalm 68:11

When Bob Huffman began deputation to go to France, he visited every pastor in East Tennessee, and it was said of him that "he turned over every stone." This characteristic stayed with him, and in order to reach others for Christ, he used every means imaginable. As mentioned earlier, two methods that were used to reach others with the Gospel were Bible posters and sandwich men. In addition, concerts were organized, Christian films were projected, and debates on subjects such as abortion were advertized, and experts in various fields were asked to share their views.

One of the most effective means of reaching those who were searching for a meaning to life was the recorded telephone message. Bob invested in the necessary equipment and every week like clock work, he prepared a short message lasting three minutes, practiced it, and then recorded it so those who called regularly would have a new message. In order to reach the general public with these messages, he would put a tiny ad in the local newspapers reading only, "Listen to the Good News,"

CHAPTER 6: EVANGELISM

followed by the phone number. Some weeks there would be over a hundred phone calls, and he always rejoiced in the number who heard. In addition, he had very small flyers measuring 1½ x 2 inches in printed up with "Listen to the Good News" and the phone number and would take the young people out to shopping centers or parking lots where they put these flyers on the car windshields.

Bible Stand

Another means of getting God's Word into the hands of the public was by having a Bible/Book stand at the open market once a week. Bob designed two large wooden suitcases that opened into display cases and had them built, covered the inside with velvet wall-paper, then filled them with Bibles and Christian books and tracts, and every Friday morning went early to set up his stand at the open market. For the market, he had to have what they called a "Patente" from city hall allowing him to sell his books, and it had to be renewed every year. Physically it was not easy because he suffered from the cold weather and had great difficulty finding shoes or boots that kept his feet warm, and socially because he always was reticent about trying to sell things; he was not a natural salesman. However, he persisted for several years.

Bible Exposition

Every few years, Bob would contact someone who had what we call a "Bible exposition" in French, and ask to borrow it for a week or two. Two or three times he asked for permission to use the public room called the "Salle St Just" on a main road in town. He would set up tables, cover them with attractive tablecloths, then organize panels with explanations and illustrations of the books of the Bible starting with Genesis and finishing with Revelation. There were also cardboard panels with verses, as well as drawings and quotations about the Bible by famous men. The exposition was open all day and evening, and the public was invited, not only to take the time to read and look over all the information, but also to fill out a questionnaire at the end, allowing them to receive a free book or New Testament. At the inauguration of each exposition, the mayor and other city dignitaries were invited and a nice Bible was presented to each one.

The mayor, Robert Montdargent, expressed his pleasure in receiving his copy, indicating that he was a "bibliophile" and possessed an impressive collection of books.

Because of these expositions, several hundred people were exposed to the Word of God. One man, of Jewish descent, came in out of curiosity, and at

CHAPTER 6: EVANGELISM

the end stopped and, with obvious emotion, told Bob he was so surprised to learn about the history of the Jews which he did not know, because during World War II he had been placed in a Catholic family and brought up Catholic. He was so touched upon learning all this that he went back through the whole exposition. Bob invited him to services and he attended once or twice, but had been drinking heavily for years and couldn't give up the habit.

A woman who taught a catechism class at the Catholic Church came out of curiosity and was so impressed that she returned with her whole family and went through a second time, then came again with the children in her catechism class and went through a third time. Many others expressed their surprise after learning much about the Bible that they had never heard. I wish I could say that many of these folks came to the church and gave their hearts and life to Christ; only a few came but didn't remain faithful.

Others reacted in different ways. One day I was standing outside inviting passersby to visit the exposition. One man, to whom I gave a tract and invitation, made a remark about not needing God or the Bible. I replied, "The Lord loves you anyway!" He stopped, and with a shocked look on his face, turned around and went the other way. I've always wondered if he ever found out just how much God does love him!

Tract Distribution

The printed page has always been one of the most effective means to share the Gospel, and Bob realized its importance. From the beginning he ordered thousands of tracts and distributed them in mailboxes, sometimes with men of the church or the youth group. One of the great burdens on his heart was the fact that so few of the French people owned a Bible, or had one in their homes, nor ever read the Bible. In fact, a woman came one day to ask for a Bible, saying that she had asked her Catholic priest for one, and he told her it was no use – for she couldn't understand it anyway! Bob not only gave her a Bible, but also explained the way to becoming a true believer. She began coming to services and accepted Christ not long after. Her three teenagers also came with her, and made professions of faith.

For several years some of the ladies went out every Thursday afternoon to distribute tracts in mailboxes. In areas where there were houses it was relatively easy – it just took a lot of walking and occasionally being frightened by a barking dog. However, in areas where there were apartments, the mailboxes were inside the main entrance and only residents had access. Many times we would ring on the interphone and ask for access, which often was refused. Other times we would wait a few minutes until someone either came out or went in,

CHAPTER 6: EVANGELISM

and catch the door. We knew that school children came home just after 4:30 P.M. and that there would be parents going in and out to go get the children and bring them home, so often we waited until then.

Distributing tracts in mailboxes

Occasionally we would have someone who had received a tract with the church name and address either call or come, but unfortunately there were few results from the tracts. Our prayer, as we placed each one in a mailbox, was not only that it would be read, but also that it would be saved, picked up again later and re-read, so that hearts and lives would be changed!

Free Bibles

The burden for getting God's Word into the hands of the people never faded but was intensified as time went on. Bob learned that he could have New Testaments in great quantity for a very reasonable price with a special cover highlighting Argenteuil, including a special message on the first page. He shared this burden with our supporters; several gifts came in, and he was able to have 28,000 printed, which amounted to a couple of tons. Fortunately, the delivery date was set ahead of time so that some of the men and youth could help unload the truck and stack the boxes. The youth group spent many hours helping us, and one weekend Brant and Maylou Holladay, our European director at that time spent an afternoon stamping and stuffing.

Since he never did anything haphazardly, Bob procured a large map of Argenteuil and tacked it on the wall outside his office. As the distribution began, each person was asked to indicate on the map which streets had been covered, thus avoiding duplication.

The reactions were numerous and varied as the citizens of Argenteuil began receiving their copies of the New Testament. One woman called to say how much she appreciated it and that the Catholics should be doing that, as well. A man

CHAPTER 6: EVANGELISM

called using inappropriate language to say he had no use for God's Word and that he didn't appreciate receiving such in his mailbox. Someone brought his copy to the church, tore its pages out and scattered them all over the street out front. Another woman called to thank us for her copy and told us she found several other copies that had been thrown away and was going to give them to the children in her catechism class. One person even brought several copies back to the Church after finding them discarded next to the mailboxes in his apartment building.

Using the air waves was another means of sharing the message of God's love, so for several years our church sponsored a radio program of twenty minutes produced by "Radio Evangile" which is aired on Sunday mornings at 8:45. It is one of the few Gospel programs that can be heard in the Paris area because the air waves are controlled by the government. Since it is heard on a private station, there is more freedom in choice of programs.

Bible Conferences

Bob also felt that the Christians needed to be "fed" and needed fellowship with Christians from other churches. For many years several of us attended a Bible Conference in the fall at Palaiseau, south of Paris. One year the organizers were not able to rent a large room or hall, so, since we were on the opposite side of the Paris conglomerate, we decided to have an annual Bible Conference in the northern suburbs, but in the spring. We were able to rent a large room from city hall, complete with chairs, a piano, loud-speakers, and some potted plants and small trees for decoration. Pastors from area churches got together to pray and plan, they chose a theme, contacted a special speaker, and made arrangements for a team to prepare a special program for the children. Each church represented was asked to participate by preparing special music as well. These conferences were held for many years, and when the rental fees became too expensive, they were transferred to our church in Argenteuil. All of God's people benefitted from the message, the music and the fellowship.

CHAPTER 7: WORKING WITH CHILDREN AND YOUTH

"And these words, which I command thee this day, shall be in thine heart: And thou shalt teach them diligently unto thy children..."
Deuteronomy 6:6,7

From the beginning of the work in the ZUP (Urban Zone) we emphasized the need to reach the children with the Gospel and to teach them God's Word. During the week we had a Bible Club, - on Wednesday afternoons at first – and taught them Bible stories, biographies of missionaries, Bible verses and songs. When we moved to the house on rue du Coq, Bob would go back and pick up children from the apartment buildings and bring them to our garage/chapel. For a while we had a really good group of 20-30 children, many of them from Algerian, Moroccan and Tunisian families. One day the van came back empty. Someone had visited all the parents in the apartments and told them their children should be learning Arabic, not Bible stories, so the children were not allowed to return.

We were thankful that Child Evangelism Fellowship materials were being translated and published in French, so we had a good selection

HIS HAND IN OUR LIVES

available. Later the Bible Clubs material became available in French, and even later we found the Awana workbooks in French published in Canada. So, for the last thirty some years we had Awana Clubs for both grammar-school-age and adolescents. The Adopt-a-Club program helped us get started since at the time the church funds were limited. Each child has a workbook at his age level and we break into small groups to learn and recite Bible verses. There are also questions to answer and the little ones can color the illustrations. By having these groups more counselors are needed, therefore more of our Christians are involved. Not only the children learn the verses in this way, and members of the "team" are called on to lead the songs, tell the story, teach a memory verse, or perhaps, man the puppets.

Over The Years

Over the years we have found that the youth who come up attending the Awana Club are the ones who grow up to be faithful members that accept responsibilities, have a heart to serve the Lord, take part in church activities and have a good testimony both in the church, at home, or out in the world. Back in 1971 when we had our first Bible Clubs in the high-rise apartments, we started with the family of six girls plus our two and it gradually expanded as others were invited. The second oldest girl, Marie-Camille, saw the need to reach other

CHAPTER 7: WORKING WITH CHILDREN

areas where the children had never heard. As she got older, she felt led of the Lord to hold Bible Clubs in the open-air during the school vacations. I remember one year in February, during the winter vacation, it was extremely cold and we had snow, ice, and below freezing temperatures the entire week. Marie-Camille did not give up or get discouraged. She went out every day with her illustrated stories, songs, and verses, and faithfully taught God's Word to the children in the playgrounds. Sometimes there were children who made fun of her, threw sand at her, or jeered, but she didn't give up! Now as an adult and mother of two girls, she continues to hold Bible Clubs, but in an orphanage in Paris. She has been an inspiration to us!

Singing with the children in Awana Club

Five-day Clubs

For several summers in August, we invited a team of two-three young people from CEF (CHILD EVANGELISM FELLOWSHIP) to come and hold 5-day clubs in our town. These youth had just finished training sessions and put their newly acquired knowledge to work. And work they did! Bob lined up four or five clubs a day in order to reach a maximum of children. There are several playgrounds between the high-rise apartments and not many of these children could go away on vacation, so they were glad to have some new and different diversions. We were always thankful that the weather was clear since all the clubs were held outside. The children were responsive and we didn't have trouble from the parents, but more than once employees from town hall questioned us, and a couple of times told us we had to have permission to do open-air work, and asked the team to leave. I can't begin to estimate how many children, and even parents who sometimes listened, heard the Gospel, but we know God's Word was proclaimed faithfully!

One of the team members the first year was a young lady from New Zealand who had heard and answered the Lord's call to France. Wendy was a special person and we appreciated having her in our home. Since she didn't know where to go after the week of 5-day clubs, we invited her to stay on with

CHAPTER 7: WORKING WITH CHILDREN

us while she sought the Lord's will. During this time she started a Bible club among the Gypsy children in a camp out away from town, taught Sunday school and made illustrated verses and songs. She stayed 4 months with us and was a blessing and an inspiration. She went on to become a well-known and well-loved children's worker in a large church in Paris. She has also written a book on reaching children for Christ, as well as headed up the organization of many special meetings for children. At this writing, she continues to serve the Lord in this capacity.

Another young lady who worked many years in our Awana club and camps was Janine. She found the Lord after a trip to Canada and began coming to services. My husband began having personal Bible studies with her, and later, she studied for a year at the Bible Institute. While helping with the Awana Club, she used puppets to tell the stories or review, which the children loved. It kept their attention and many truths were shared and driven home in their hearts. She was also much appreciated as a counselor at camp with us and Pastor Dédéyan. The camp ministry has been an additional means of reaching the young. For many years we worked as counselors at "Le Camp de la Bonne Nouvelle" (The Good News Camp) with Pasteur Dédéyan. The camp is located in southern France near the Spanish border, thus giving the children and youth the possibility of enjoying warm weather, while swimming and sleeping in tents. Every morning we had a Bible study for each of the different age groups, and an evangelistic service every evening. Many young souls were awakened to their need of a Savior and gave their hearts to the Lord. Others, already Christian, saw the need to consecrate their life to serving Him. It has been rewarding to return later and find former campers now grown up and faithful to the Lord. Some even returned as counselors; others send their children to the camp each summer. Statistically, it is the best way to reach youth with the message of Christ's love and forgiveness.

The Good News Camp

CHAPTER 7: WORKING WITH CHILDREN

Winter Snow Camps

Very few of our youth in Argenteuil have the opportunity to learn to ski or even play in the snow. Early in the ministry we followed the Lord's leading and organized Snow Camps which took place during the winter school vacation First, we planned everything on paper; including the menus, the Bible studies, the games, the evening messages, teams to help with cleanup, and the amount each one needed to share expenses. By doing almost everything ourselves, we were able to keep the price low. Bob called different areas to find a suitable chalet with room for about 25. We purchased and took with us everything for meals except fresh French bread, fresh fruit and frozen foods. Thus, the vehicles were packed to the hilt. In this way the men could spend more time with the youth instead of looking for groceries. The young ones loved every minute of camp, and were so happy to ski, ride sleds or even just make a snowman. Therefore, every year after Christmas they began asking "Are we going to have a winter camp this year? Even some adults went and enjoyed the activities as much as the youth. Now that Bob is gone, no one has taken on the responsibility of carrying on, and all those who went regret this very much. It was the highlight of the long, cold winter.

Helpers

Not long before we moved into town and rented "this old house," a young woman came by the office and asked about our meetings. She also inquired about our doctrines and beliefs. Madame Bezuel had been meeting with a small group that had relocated and was seeking a church home and a Christian family. Learning that the Bible was preached faithfully, she began attending with her three children. Because she had experience in teaching any and all ages, she soon became one of our most faithful and well-loved teachers. Her joyful personality overflowed to the adult members as well as the children. Her burden for souls was so profound that people were drawn to her and she faithfully shared God's love and His Word with all. It was a sad day for us when her husband retired and they moved to Brittany, several hours away.

Many other members have worked with the children in Sunday school, Bible Club and Awana Club. This has helped our young people grow spiritually as they hear or prepare the lessons, the songs which have a real message, the verses that the children memorize, and the missionary adventures. We have encouraged young Christians to help with children's and youth work, because we always need to help them grasp the basic truths and doctrines in God's Word.

CHAPTER 7: WORKING WITH CHILDREN

Studying God's Word

Youth Group

Sharing the Good News of Christ's love and sacrifice with young people was a primary concern for Bob, and right from the start we invited teens and young adults into our home in the ZUP. At first we asked those who were interested in English conversation to come, thus allowing us to make contact. Then, in addition to English we added a meeting during which we played games such as "Rhythm" to break the ice and allow the youth to become somewhat acquainted. A devotion at their level followed, and a question and answer time was an important part. When we moved from our apartment to the house on rue du Coq, we continued the youth group, adding a ping-pong table since we had a basement. Dealing with immorality among these teens was an important part in reaching them, for having sexual experience was status quo. One mother told me she was concerned about her older son of 16 who had no girlfriend while his younger brother was already promiscuous. Waiting until marriage was not an option for them.

Meeting Others

In order to meet other Christian youth, Bob often took our youth to special meetings in area churches. This is how our daughter Licia met the young man who was to become her life partner. They were 16 when they met, and began a relationship that continued by phone calls and letters over a period of three or four years. When Licia returned from a year of study in the US, she began medical school in Orsay, southwest of Paris. Pascal's studies in agronomy at a nearby university gave them the opportunity to see each other and get to know one another. They became engaged and began planning their wedding for October 1989.

As our teens finished high school, went on to the university and out to finding work, they were too mature to remain in the youth group. We began a group of young adults which met on Sunday

CHAPTER 7: WORKING WITH CHILDREN

afternoons, and continued guiding them in their spiritual lives. Meeting with others their age was as important for them as for the teens, so the area pastors began having an all-day conference for them on November 11th which is a holiday, and included the young adults from all area churches. These meetings were especially appreciated and well-attended, and later, all day sporting events were planned so they could get together more often. Out of this group have come several who went to the Bible Institute, not to mention several couples that formed and were married. Now the majority of them have little ones that are growing up knowing the Lord!

Bible Studies

As the young adults grew and matured spiritually, several felt the Lord would have them go to one of the Bible Institutes to gain a deeper understanding and knowledge of the Bible. Bob encouraged them all to take a year off from their studies, either the year following high school or after university studies, before making application for a position or job. He always told our youth that they should aim for the highest in using their capacities and talents the Lord gave them. Over a period of almost forty years, twelve of our young people have spent at least a year at a Bible Institute. Of these, three went for one year, two are still studying, two became pastors but did not continue in this ministry, two went to night school so were not full-time students, and three became pastors or evangelists and are still serving the Lord.

Music

Praising the Lord through music is always an important part of worship. When we began holding our meetings in our apartment, we sang *a cappella* for lack of instruments. Not long after our move to a house, I received news that my grandfather had passed away, leaving a small sum of money to each of his grands and great-grands. We invested the greater part in bonds with interest for the future studies of the three children, then invested the rest in a good used piano so they could begin learning to play. The piano was installed in the chapel to be used not only for practices, but also for the services when someone who could play was present.

Lauri began learning to play some of the hymns to accompany the singing, and later on Patricia, who played the accordion, used her talent for the Lord. When the Albain family became members, their children added much to the services, playing the violin, the flute and the electric piano. There was also Pierre Celestin, an excellent guitarist, who not only played but composed as well. His wife Sylvie was from a musical family, and sang beautifully. Claude Samson, another talented member, played the

CHAPTER 7: WORKING WITH CHILDREN

guitar, composed, and practiced for the singing. He also sang with his wife, Chantal.

Accompaniment

Once we moved into the renovated building behind our house in town, a choir was formed and directed by Jean Albain and was under his direction for many years. It was a real blessing, not only to sing God's praises, but also to have the fellowship at practice time and to be able to contribute to the time of worship. After Jean retired, no one took over immediately, so when Eric and Stephanie moved into the area, we were glad to have Stephanie, who is a music professor, re-organize the choir. Unfortunately, she only stayed with us three or four years, so she was greatly missed when Eric left for the Bible Institute in Algrange.

Several of the mothers have worked with the children, teaching them special songs for Christmas, Easter, Mothers 'Day, etc. These last few years Roland has taken on the responsibility of planning for the time of praise just before the eleven o'clock service. He asks different young folks, families or individuals to lead the praise time which helps keep the rhythm steady and aids in learning new songs.

Jean Albain's children all played an instrument, and from the time they began coming to services, they always added much to the service, not only in accompaniment, but with special music, as well. Thierry played the flute and later the saxophone; Claudine the violin and piano, and Caroline the electric piano. Our daughter, Leanne, who was about their age, also played the piano, so we often had all four of them practicing before church, or on Saturday afternoons after youth group met. As other young people became proficient, they joined our small orchestra, and now, since we have several who play the piano, they take turns playing for the praise service and for church. There is Barbara, Anne-Evelyne, Ingrid, Jennifer, who also plays the flute, and Julina, who plays the violin very well. We do have one young man who plays the guitar, and we would like to see other guys come alongside and learn an instrument. We have sent up much praise to the Lord because of such talent being used to glorify Him!

Called to serve

René, one of our faithful men, was a male nurse at the hospital in Argenteuil, and because of his testimony and invitations, several colleagues began attending services and hearing the Gospel. One by one, as they came to know the Lord, they shared their faith with those around them. In all, six or seven professed Christ. Since part of them were student nurses, they went elsewhere to work after receiving their diplomas. René also shared his faith with athletes he knew, due to the fact that he

CHAPTER 7: WORKING WITH CHILDREN

had been a champion tennis player before giving his life to serve the Lord. One of them was Jocelyn, a referee for the soccer team in town. Jocelyn didn't take René seriously at first, but as he watched his life he became convinced that René was different. One Sunday morning he got up, got dressed and came to the services. He said later that the message Bob preached was aimed directly at him, and he became a believer after realizing how far from pleasing to the Lord his life was.

A Changed Life

Jocelyn began coming regularly to services and asked to be baptized. Bob went to visit him and learned he was living with Daniella but they were not married. So Bob talked with her, explained what Christ had done on the cross, and she also professed Christ as her Lord. Bob explained that it would be a good testimony if they got married first and were baptized afterwards. They agreed, so began planning their wedding. It was a joyous time for both their family and their new-found Christian family! Their two children, Johan and Julie, also began coming to Sunday school and Bible Club, and have remained faithful all these years, as have their parents. A few years later the Lord gave them Josué, a third child, to bring up in the faith from the start. Jocelyn's mother, Suzanne, also came to know the Lord; we are still praying for his dad and several of his brothers and sisters. Bob saw a lot of potential in Jocelyn, therefore he encouraged him to serve the Lord in spite of his hesitation. He began studying the Bible on his own, and later took special courses to work with an organization entitled "Famille Je T'aime" (I love families). At the writing of these lines, he still goes to churches in the area and all over France to speak in conferences on the family. He also is a deacon in the church, has special classes to prepare couples for marriage, and teaches the class for new converts and those who have asked for baptism. In 2014 there were ten baptized.

As for René, he completed his training as a male nurse, took further training to be a supervisor, and eventually returned to his native island of Guadeloupe in the West Indies, married Patricia from his church, and, in addition to his duties at the hospital, holds evangelistic meetings in churches all over the islands and in France when he comes to visit. He has been used of the Lord to win many to Christ. His brother, Alain, is pastor of a church in the area north of Paris.

Others showed promise of becoming full-time workers for the Lord such as Jean-Luc. He married one of the girls from church and they had a little girl, but while they were on vacation, his cousin seduced his wife, and even after counseling and much prayer, they got a divorce. Jean-Luc was so deeply hurt by unfounded accusations that he has

CHAPTER 7: WORKING WITH CHILDREN

never returned to church. Seeing him abandon the Lord has been especially difficult for Bob who was discipling Jean-Luc, as well as for his mother who is one of our most faithful ladies.

Twice Forgiven

Another was Jean-Claude, who completed three years at the Bible Institute and felt called to serve the Lord as a pastor. He was one of those reached indirectly by the testimony of René. A neighbor of a nurse at the hospital, he showed interest in the Christian life when she spoke with him about the meetings. She gave Bob his phone number, so Bob called and made an appointment to visit in his home. He made a profession of faith and began attending services. One day he asked Bob to go by his place to talk, and when he arrived, Jean-Claude had a huge travel bag sitting in the living room. He explained that he worked in town and one of his buddies worked in security at another store and could turn off the machine that rang if one tried to slip out without paying. He had made it a habit of acquiring CD's by asking his friend to turn it off a few minutes so he could slip out, and the bag was full and running over with the unpaid-for CD's. The Holy Spirit had convicted him about this and showed him this was stealing, and he wanted to make it right without going to jail. After much prayer, Bob took the travel bag, contacted the store director and made an appointment, and explained that Jean-Claude wanted to make things right because he had become a Christian. The director was understanding and agreed not to press charges because the CD's had been returned and he wanted to give him a chance to make a new start. He became one of our most faithful young men, and after graduating from the Bible Institute, the men of the church asked him to help out with the young people. Bob was grooming him to become assistant pastor when Jean-Claude suddenly announced he was leaving for Africa as a missionary. It was learned later that he had been dating a young lady from our church in spite of her parents' refusal because of her age, and the parents had found this out. In Africa things didn't work out, so he returned, asked forgiveness of the family and the church, pastored a small church briefly, and now attends a church faithfully with his family while working a secular job.

Be Faithful

One of the biggest disappointments in Bob's ministry was the fact that so many who felt called to serve and began preparing fell by the wayside. It was hard for him to understand why they were not persistent and faithful to their call and to their Lord. We saw so many of our beloved French people, both young and old, come for a while then fall away, either because of indifference to the Gospel or because of the pull of the attractions of the

CHAPTER 7: WORKING WITH CHILDREN

world. Bob realized how important it was for each new Christian to study God's Word regularly and to establish a personal relationship with the Lord. He often repeated from the pulpit the admonition we heard over and over while at the Bible Institute: "Be faithful, young people, be faithful," which was the favorite saying of Dr. Lee Roberson.

CHAPTER 8: THIS OLD HOUSE

"Behold, your house is left unto you desolate."
Matthew 23:38

Our five years in the house on rue du Coq were not only eventful but very enjoyable, especially for the children. All three played in the backyard, as well as with the children who lived on our street. We would have stayed there longer if the Lord hadn't taken drastic measures to move us out! In March, we had our plane tickets in hand and were ready to leave for furlough in a week when our landlord came knocking on the door to deliver some upsetting news! He needed his house to provide shelter for two elderly aunts. Could we be out by June so he could begin renovations? It was as if he had dropped a bomb!

Bob invited him in to talk and explained our situation to him, asking for an extension to the beginning of August. He agreed, and we were able to leave as planned, but scheduled our date of return one month earlier to house-hunt. The Lindquist's, who were going to Senegal as soon as they finished language training, gave up their apartment and moved into our house in order to

CHAPTER 8: THIS OLD HOUSE

assure the doors were open for the services. While we were absent, they began looking for suitable places to rent or buy.

To No Avail

As we traveled in the US, we shared the need for a larger meeting place. The Lord had encouraged us by an attendance of over 50 the Sunday before we left. Our desire was to purchase a building suitable to house the church and our family, therefore we shared with the American churches and supporters what we thought was God's will and most reasonable choice for allowing expansion of the ministry.

We had been searching for three weeks after returning to France, when finally the agencies began opening late in August and we were able to see what was available. Choices were few because in 1977 a change in the government policies had greatly discouraged rentals. The first week of September, a large house was put up for rent, and even though it was in very poor shape, we felt we had to take it. Bob still felt there was something more suitable out there, and that this would only be temporary. Before moving in, however, he rented a sander to clean the floors in the living and dining rooms, and put a couple coats of varnish on them. Vandals had broken in and drawn with chalk on the aging wall-paper, water had seeped in around the fireplaces, the electric installations were so old that many of the wires were covered only with cloth, and the drain from the shower upstairs ran down the outside and was subject to freezing in winter. The ceilings were a grimy gray with crooked lines of fresh white plaster where the cracks had been filled. Even though we weren't sure of staying there, we had to do a minimum to clean it up.

So, we paid the required 3 months rent deposit and asked the owner if we could move in early so our children could start school. (We couldn't enroll them earlier because we had no permanent address!) He agreed, making sure we realized that the electrician would be installing new wiring and bringing the electricity up to norms. Little by little, we brought our furniture in, including the folding chairs and a portable pulpit for the service. It took time to get the gas, telephone, etc. turned on, inform everyone of our new address and have our mail forwarded. Slowly we made progress, but then Bob had to go to Germany for a missions conference in an American military church for 4-5 days.

Three Coats of Paint

Swante Lindquist was still staying with us, sleeping in his van since we were short on beds. He had helped immensely with moving the furniture and cleaning. After Bob left, he went and purchased

CHAPTER 8: THIS OLD HOUSE

several gallons of white paint, and one by one painted the ceilings. It took three coats to cover the gray, but what a change it made! The day Bob left I came down with the flu, and I was so sick I stayed in bed most of the time for 3-4 days. Swante helped with the children, who were ages 14, 10, 7 and 2, and even prepared the meals.

Our desire to find something more suitable did not become reality, for even though Bob checked for several months, there was hardly anything for rent at that time. Homeowners were selling, not renting. Because a woman's home is an extension of herself, I became more and more uncomfortable living in the old place, and dreamed of a place of our own with a yard for the children. The girls didn't want to invite their friends over because their bedroom was such a disgrace, and Bob didn't want to take the time to redo it. He knew that if we began in one room we would have to do the others too! In the spring he was off to another conference for several days. The girls and I walked downtown and together and picked out some wallpaper that would easily cover the old. We had already scrubbed the painted woodwork and it was in pretty good shape, so we learned to cut the lengths and the three of us re-papered the whole room. At last it was clean!

When Bob returned we showed him our handiwork and he was surprised and proud of our initiative. He was also glad it was done and that he didn't have to do it! He was right about needing to do the other rooms, but by then he was resigned, since we had started work on the basement.

After that we re-did his office, and during the summer the living dining room, then painted the kitchen. As time went on we did the bathrooms, hallway and our bedroom.

A House Church

For our church meetings, we pushed the dining room table over to the side, opened the French doors between the living-dining room and lined chairs up facing the pulpit in both rooms. It was crowded, but we were thankful to have a meeting place! Bob's office served as a Sunday school room, so we were able to continue teaching the children. We even presented a Christmas program that year! But it was clear that we needed more room in a place that was set aside specifically for our meetings. New contacts didn't always feel at ease, especially in the evenings when we had Bible studies. The only place that was larger than our living-dining room was the basement, and it didn't seem promising because the "floor" was packed dirt and our heads almost touched the ceiling. Before we made any plans, we took the idea to the Lord, then asked the owner for permission to not only dig out and pour a cement floor, but also to knock out

CHAPTER 8: THIS OLD HOUSE

the wall below the window to make room for a door and to pour cement steps leading down to it. Any improvements were to his advantage in the long run. He gave us permission, so we announced the project to the church members and asked them to take time out to help, and began digging. To evacuate the dirt, Bob took the seats out of the Volkswagen bus, put a thick plastic canvas on the floor and up the sides, and loaded it up. He made 17 trips to the dump before the space was adequate in height, plus a few inches to allow for the cement floor. Even though he did most of the work by himself, he had a few helpers: the girls from youth group including our oldest daughter Lauri. She not only helped dig out, but poured cement, as well!

Once the floor was dry, a carpenter friend from England put up wall paneling. To cover the large water evacuation pipes, we made a huge curtain of gold-colored upholstery material. Bob rented an air hammer and we enlarged the window we had been using to take the dirt out in order to make room for the door. The son of one of our faithful ladies came and measured the space, made a door just the right size, and then spent several days pouring cement steps down to the entrance. We were then able to move our meetings downstairs, out of our living quarters. Neon lights were installed, plus a smaller curtain to cover the

HIS HAND IN OUR LIVES

stairs leading up to the kitchen. For insulation we put in carpeting both on the floor and the stairs.

The finished product made an acceptable, if modest, meeting room. There was easily room for 60 plus in attendance, and we continued to hold the Sunday school classes in the living room and office. Now we had room to grow, which we did, although slowly. The basement room was also used for Bible Club Wednesday since the children had no school that day, for Youth group on Saturday, and for Wednesday evening Bible study.

Underground Church

For several years, we met in this basement room, all the while praying that the Lord would open a door and give us a more suitable place to hold services. One day, Madame Martin was standing outside with me looking at the building behind our house. It was being used by our landlady's son-in-law for his business and employees. We decided that we would pray together that the business would prosper so greatly that they would need larger and more adequate offices and workroom. A few months later he told Bob that he would be moving to the industrial zone in order to have more space plus easier access and much needed parking spaces. The Lord had answered our prayer! So Bob contacted the owner about renting the building which had enough space

CHAPTER 8: THIS OLD HOUSE

for about 100 people, a nursery, office, and Sunday school class. Soon the papers were signed and we were able to begin renovations, all the while thanking and praising God for His positive answer.

This old house: the church building is behind

Since the work was so involved, we contacted John Abuhl, an American Christian living in France, who was in construction and did renovations for churches as a ministry. He agreed to come, and for several months he worked on insulating the building completely, building a platform, installing a more attractive door in the entry, adding baseboards, and finally, painting. Some of the ladies came to help with varnishing and painting. We were able to dedicate and move into the building six months

HIS HAND IN OUR LIVES

later and what a blessing it was to have room to move around in! It was while we were in this building that the church really grew and became an established work, registered with the government as a religious assembly.

Thieves!

Living in town was convenient for shopping and school activities, but there were often unpredictable happenings which kept us on our toes. When our landlord had his workshop out back, much of his stock of bathroom accessories (towel racks, etc) was displayed on the ground floor. Evidently some of his workers left the front door unlocked because things began disappearing. One day Bob saw a man exiting the workroom with an orange crate piled high with merchandise. He asked him about it, and realizing it was stolen, ordered him to put it back. The boss came down from his office upstairs, saw what was going on, took the crate and told the man to get out and never come back or he would call the police. From then on we locked all doors at all times. One Saturday when Leanne went out back for youth group she forgot to lock the kitchen door. I was in the office with an English student and heard the door click, but didn't pay much attention. Later when I went out, I got my purse from the back of the door to the kitchen and saw my billfold with all my papers was missing. After searching the house and asking the family

CHAPTER 8: THIS OLD HOUSE

what they knew, I realized what had taken place, and checked the back door. Sure enough, it was unlocked. On Monday I went down the street to the police station to report the theft and to procure temporary ID papers. The young woman who typed my information especially understood, and, as I often did, I gave her a thank-you tract upon leaving, and invited her to services. She asked me about meetings for children, and wanted to bring her daughter, aged 10. The following Sunday she was present; her daughter began coming to the Bible club, and accepted the Lord. Mother and daughter came regularly for several months before she was transferred to another town. Seeing the good that came after having my billfold stolen made the verse in Romans 8:28 all the more meaningful to me!

    The word had gotten around among the homeless that there was merchandise to be had, so we became even more cautious about locking doors. They even stole our welcome mat off the front steps. Bob's office was upstairs in the church building, and one morning while he was studying, he heard noise, so quietly cracked his door to look out. A fellow was upstairs looking around so he yelled "What are you doing?" The guy jumped and then ran downstairs with Bob right behind him, and he and another guy ran out the front door and out the driveway to the street. Bob turned back,

HIS HAND IN OUR LIVES

realizing he couldn't catch them, and locked the door. Upon checking around, he found that they had unplugged the complete sound system and set it aside to take it with them, plus other items. He thanked the Lord for preventing them from getting away with it, as replacing it would have been very expensive for our little group. It was surprising that they operated in broad daylight, but an even greater surprise was awaiting us. One Saturday the choir was at church practicing on the platform, and some members had left personal belongings on the chairs near the front. Two young men wandered in and we greeted them, asking them to come back for service. They said they liked our music and asked if they could stay and listen. All of a sudden one of them walked out, and Sami jumped down and took off after him when he saw his attaché case was gone. And the race was on! Down the street, across the center of the crossroads, in front of the store and into the park they raced! When the thief saw that Sami was gaining on him, he threw down the case and continued running. Sami was thankful to have it back, because it contained his French ID and other important papers. From that time on, he kept his personal belongings with him, and we didn't have other visitors come in off the street as we practiced.

CHAPTER 8: THIS OLD HOUSE

A Neighbor Boy

Only one other incident of stealing occurred, and that was while we were in the US on furlough. Someone broke into our house and took a couple pieces of gold jewelry plus tried to crack an old safe that was in the house when we rented it. We assumed there was nothing of value stored there since it was abandoned, and we had no combination. "They" weren't able to open it either, although we wished they had so we wouldn't "wonder" anymore. Years later someone took a sledge hammer and broke open one of the two compartments, but only found several books of check stubs dating back to the 1930's. Lance, who had helped do some digging for artifacts on a couple of sites in Argenteuil, took them to the historical society where they were used to learn more about the history of the town. Many years later, a neighbor boy, Frederic, found out we had moved, looked us up and came to see us. In reminiscing he confessed that he had climbed to the roof of the church meeting room, gone over to our bedroom window and worked it open, took the jewelry and tried to get into the safe. To him it was funny. We didn't really know what to say except "Some day the Lord will judge you—" He immediately changed the subject, not wanting to speak of spiritual things.

CHAPTER 9: BURSTING AT THE SEAMS

"Be like-minded, having the same love, being of one accord..." Philippians 2:2

Even though we enlarged the meeting room and used every bit of space we had, we were still crowded. Our congregation continued to grow, which meant more children, more youth, and nowhere to expand! Not only was the church building used, but also our house was filled with different Sunday school classes: Primaries in the living room, juniors in the basement, adolescents in the office, and we even had a class of girls in the kitchen for a while!

For several years, the church council had been putting aside a percentage of the offerings to purchase a larger building for our meetings and activities. Not only were we growing in number, our youth and children were growing up! The children were becoming adolescents, the adolescents were developing into young adults, and the young couples were having babies! The men of the church kept their eyes open for a large building in the area which might be made into a suitable place to meet. Nothing was available for a long time, so we

CHAPTER 9: BURSTING AT THE SEAMS

continued praying, inviting folks to church or special meetings, and training the Christians for service to the LORD.

Bob and I were especially aware of the need to train our Christians to take on responsibility and dedicate time and effort to the Lord's work. Not only did we feel the need for helpers, but we were getting older, and couldn't keep up with the young folks as well! Terry and Patsy Arp had to leave North Africa where they had served many years for health reasons, and they came alongside in Argenteuil and worked with us until they were able to start a work out farther away from the Paris suburbs. It was a joy to have their support in the ministry and we greatly enjoyed the fellowship, as well. Our children had a good time with theirs when we had time to get together and relax.

Preparing For The Future

Early on in our ministry, Bob realized and saw from experience that those who did studies in preparation for their baptism became more faithful Christians than those who did not. Therefore, he found a series of studies that each person could do at home, then asked them to come to his office so they could go over each lesson together and make sure they understood. Not only did this give them a solid basis in living the Christian life, but a relationship developed between shepherd and sheep, which was important. He was especially close to his young people, whom he saw up through Awana clubs, adolescents group, youth and young adults' class, and called the young ladies "his girls." He was very protective of them, and his great desire was to see them stay faithful to God, and remain pure until their marriage. One of "his girls" came to me during his final illness and asked if he could baptize her. It was a great disappointment for her to learn that in the last stages he could hardly get out of bed, so her "papa" spiritual was not able to baptize her. It took her over two years to get over this and finally follow the Lord in baptism.

As the years went by and the youth grew up, they started to form couples and make marriage plans. Bob made an appointment with each couple and suggested that they follow lessons on preparation to marriage before tying the knot. If one of our young people became engaged to someone outside the church, Bob's main concern was that he/she knew the Lord. He made a rendezvous with them and presented the Gospel. In this way several came to know Christ and the couple was an "equal yoke"; could have a full relationship spiritually as well as physically, and could bring their children up in a Christian home. If one of the couple did not know the Lord and did not see the need to follow and live for Christ, he could not in good conscience bless them during a

CHAPTER 9: BURSTING AT THE SEAMS

religious ceremony in the church. This policy made more than one young member realize just how important it was to date and marry someone who followed Christ.

Once Jocelyn Pitkiaye became a representative for the organization, "Family, I love you" upon completing his training, he took over the classes of preparation for marriage. He even held special meetings to introduce couples living together to "a better way" in following God's commandments. More than one faithful family in the church today came to these meetings, made profession of faith, got married and were baptized. Their children come regularly and the family is united in love and faith in God.

Because of our emphasis on reaching children for Christ, we saw the need early on for training classes to prepare workers. We asked an experienced missionary lady to come and share with us, and at the end she left her courses for us to use due to her up-coming retirement. Every three or four years, we offered the training in order to have enough workers for Awana club, Sunday school, Children's Church and summer camps. It was important to keep the need before the Christians, as well.

Since one of my main burdens was in children's ministry, I prepared lessons and did Teachers' Training classes, and shared them not only with our church folk, but also in a couple of neighboring churches. Because we had such a good group that followed the courses and received their diplomas we were able to add Children's Church which took place during the message, thus taking advantage of the time the children were with us. A few years later, when my health began to fail, we asked a couple with CEF (Child Evangelism Fellowship) to do Teacher's Training, thus continuing to add workers.

One of our most faithful Christians who helped with children's work, Denise, was not only an enthusiastic teacher and colleague, but also had much experience working with children. She took on the responsibility of helping with the training classes and was an enormous aide and encouragement. She was always optimistic, has great faith in her Lord and shares her joy in being His child with everyone. We were extremely disappointed to see her leave the area when her husband retired, and still miss her.

Another important ministry that we often shared as a couple was visitation. Bob preferred having someone with him when he made hospital calls, and often I was elected. We also visited most of our families in their homes, thus getting to know their situations, problems, other family members, as well as their spiritual needs. We became very close to our "flock"; little by little becoming one big

CHAPTER 9: BURSTING AT THE SEAMS

family that prayed together, worshipped together, helped each other, and enjoyed each other's company.

In order to encourage fellowship among Christians, Bob and the men of the council planned special outings and meetings year-round. February was usually the annual business meetings as well as a dinner and conference in a nice restaurant for couples around Valentine's Day. March was missions' month when we renewed our Faith Promise pledge for our missionaries. The new year found us making plans for our winter camp in the mountains. At first it was an outing for ados and youth, but later it became a family camp. Everyone benefitted from the mountain air, the exercise, either sledding or skiing, as well as the Bible studies mornings and messages in the evenings. The youth also learned to work together, because we divided them into teams which took turns either helping in meal preparation, setting and clearing tables, and washing the dishes, as well as keeping the chalet clean. (See chapter on "Working with children and youth" for more details).

In the spring, if weather permitted, we would have a picnic in a huge park where we could cook out, set up a net for Volleyball, play ball, walk in the woods, and relax together. Then as the school year came to a close, the Awana club kids planned a program to share with parents, etc. what they had learned during the year. Because the main thrust in Awana is memorization of God's Word, many verses were shared and awards were presented. The kids also had an end-of-the-year outing in a nearby park, with games and refreshments.

One year when the nationwide conference in Palaiseau did not take place because of lack of a meeting place, we organized an area Bible Conference in the spring, renting a large room and facilities in Argenteuil for the 3-day meetings. The men who met for the Pastoral took care of choosing a theme, finding a speaker, and designing and printing up a prospectus announcing the meetings. Invitations were sent out, not only to churches, but also to the Mayor and other important dignitaries. The town hall loaned us plants for decoration, tables for displaying Bibles, books and CDs offered for purchase by the Maison de la Bible, and even a piano for our musicians and (a sound system). The conference was held in this room for several years, and contributed greatly to promoting fellowship among the churches, propagation of God's Word, plus an opportunity to purchase good Christian literature. We organized and held the springtime Bible conference each year in Argenteuil, and were able to make a few contacts even though the theme and messages were often directed at Christians. It was a good time of fellowship and sharing burdens

CHAPTER 9: BURSTING AT THE SEAMS

with others from area churches and brought the Christians together to pray for souls. A team was formed to be responsible for the nursery and children's meetings with refreshments provided. Every year we looked forward to this time of spiritual renewal.

Ladies' Meetings

Our ladies had their get-togethers, too. Once a month we met for payer, a Bible Study, and refreshments. For a few years we had two ladies' meetings every week, the reason being some of our families were having marital troubles and I knew the wife was suffering. God's Word always has the answer, so we went to the scriptures to study the causes of a troubled family and home and the remedies. One family was helped and has a peaceful relationship; several others were fortified and the whole family is more faithful. Once or twice a year, we planned get-togethers with a theme and a speaker, and invited the ladies from other churches to join us. These meetings were especially appreciated and always well attended.

One of our young couples from Haiti had been married in our church. The wife was not saved when they asked Bob to officiate. When they came to see him, he presented the Gospel and she came sweetly to the Lord and has been a faithful Christian ever since. They had been married over two years and no baby came; her side of the family in Haiti was so worried they planned to meet and use voodoo to make her fertile. She shared this with me, so two or three of the ladies came with me and we went to her apartment and had a special prayer meeting to ask the Lord to give them a child. Two months later she shared in testimony time that the Lord had heard our prayers and that she was expecting a little one. We were overjoyed, for we knew this baby was a gift of God; not a result of voodoo chants.

Even though we took advantage of every possible means of sharing the Gospel and stirring interest so folks would come to special meetings, most of the population of Argenteuil (and France for that matter) has almost no idea of what a Baptist or a Protestant Church believe in. Many times, when people were invited, they hesitated because they had so many questions and never found the answers. Some are very suspicious of any religion!

One woman, with whom I shared my faith, had never heard the words "protestant" or "Pasteur" before. A fact that surprised us, but then that was the reason the Lord sent us to France; to share God's love, our faith, and to show those with whom we come in contact where to go to learn more!

CHAPTER 10: OUR OWN BUILDING

"...that I may go unto mine own place..."
Genesis 30:25

One of the great desires we had as a church-planting couple was to bring the church to the place where it could purchase its own building and not have to move again. We had prayed to this end for many years while waiting on the Lord. In 1999 our landlord informed us that the property, with both the house and the church, would be put up for sale. We took this news to the council and members of the church, and they agreed that the time had come to purchase a building that would allow us to have a permanent location. We had first option, of course, but there were three important drawbacks: 1) No room to grow. Already we were crowded and still reaching others. 2) Not enough space for parking. In town there was no place left to use for parking lots, so our faithful Christians had to park on the street, double-park, or ask the folks at the gas station across the street if they could park there. 3) The price of the property was much higher than in other areas of town. 4) The building the church used had important structural weaknesses.

HIS HAND IN OUR LIVES

It would take several thousand francs to stabilize the building and a lot of work. Bob and the men went to several agencies and looked at various possibilities, but most of them were just shells of a building that would take months to restore.

Finally, after looking for more than a year, a very large building was located. Built right next to the cemetary, it had served as an exposition hall for tombstones and coffins, but had been empty for years. First of all, we sought the Lord's will concerning this place, which, although it complied with several of our criteria, would need serious repairs and transformations. Bob began negotiating with the owner and then the men made an offer below the sale price but within the financial means of the church budget. It was refused. So we continued praying and looking, but nothing else was available that fit our needs. The council decided to make a more substantial offer after checking about getting a loan at the bank. More than seven months had gone by since the first offer was refused and no one else had made an offer, therefore, our second offer was accepted! We were overjoyed and praised the Lord for this answer to prayer and for His provision of this building!

It took 8 months of negotiating with the bankers, of filling out papers, and yes, of redoing them, for the bank made mistakes in which forms we needed. They had never made a loan to a

CHAPTER 10: OUR OWN BUILDING

church which was a non-profit organization before, and it was like the blind leading the blind. When things finally came together, the young man in charge of our loan at the bank was surprised to learn that it was for a French church! All along he thought it was for an American church! That struck us as funny, because we only knew of one other American living in Argenteuil, a town of over 100, 000 population.

A Building Of Our Own

Near the end of October the bank informed us that the papers were ready to be signed, and they would need several members of the church to commit themselves financially if the church failed in reimbursing the loan. Several of us were present for the signing on October 30. At last the church had a building of its own and no-one could ask us to move! The next day (October 31), a few of the men went over to the church to begin cleaning, carrying away rubbish, and make plans concerning where to start. It was decided that the largest room would be used for services, that a nursery would be walled off at the back of the building, that a wall would be added to create a hallway between classrooms and main auditorium, that a bathroom large enough for handicapped would be built, and that the 2nd largest room that needed the most work, would be used as a fellowship hall eventually to be renovated later when time and finances permitted. As with all renovations, there were surprises, such as the need to replace all the insulation above the ceiling. Bob and the men took it all out and making several trips with the church van, took it to the recycling center. The young man who worked there saw them come several times, and there was such a quantity he asked then "Are you re-doing a castle or what?"

It was decided that we would focus our attention on the main auditorium because we could only meet in our present building until January 31st. The new owner graciously allowed three months in the old building so we could get the new auditorium ready for services. Not only did our members come to work when they could, but Christians from other churches came and offered their services. Even students from the Bible institute who were qualified in renovating, came and did both bathrooms, and a pastor and his sons from Belgium came and worked almost a week, putting in a raised platform for the pulpit, and ceilings in the SS rooms.

CHAPTER 10: OUR OWN BUILDING

Our new building

First Church Service

We made the deadline, so we moved the church and Bob's office to the new quarters, and on the first Sunday in February 2001, held our first meeting in the new building. There remained an enormous amount of renovating, so we kept our work clothes out and tackled the next tasks. I worked alongside the men, and other ladies came when they could. They also contributed meals for the workers. These included a team of mostly retired folks from the US who worked two weeks, a group of American military stationed in Germany, a couple who were missionaries in England and Wales, and a man and woman from one of our supporting churches in Maryland, USA, all spending several days to work. The team from the US paid their own flights and hotel rooms!

In any kind of work, there are stumbling blocks which slow down the progress. Before beginning the renovations, we engaged an architect to help us, thus hoping to avoid any pitfalls concerning norms, etc. The hallways had to be a certain width, the bathrooms a certain dimension, the gas lines a certain height and painted a certain yellow... Just a few weeks after putting up a wall in the fellowship hall, the dimensions on the hallways changed, therefore we were obligated to take it down and move it over. Not too many other changes had to be made, so when the fire department came to inspect, there were only a few minor details to be taken care of.

His Office

The second phase of renovations was equal in the amount of work as was the first. The room that became Bob's office needed repairs on the roof before we could begin work inside. Bob and I went to look at paint and wall-paper, and he chose a traditional design of green and gold on an off-white background, with a green border. We also had to wall-paper the ceiling, which was on a slant, to

CHAPTER 10: OUR OWN BUILDING

cover the imperfections. He bought shelves and lined two walls with many volumes. When we finally moved his desk and chair in and unpacked all his boxes, he was happy as a lark! For six months he had missed having his office where he could be alone with the Lord, and study in preparation for his messages and Bible studies.

In the meantime, Bob and I had to find a place for us, as well! We had been living in "this old house" for 24 years, and had accumulated much more than we needed. We looked at a couple of 3-4 room apartments in the area, but they were not suitable. Leanne had previously given English lessons to several students younger that she, and during the summer that year had watered the plants in an empty apartment for the mother of one young girl while they were on vacation. They had bought a house seven years earlier, but kept the apartment for the mother-in-law to move into when her husband passed away. She had recently decided to stay in her house, therefore the apartment would soon be put up for sale. I went and looked at it but wanted to look at some others before deciding. When we saw what was available in our price range, we went back to look again at this apartment. Besides having 3 bedrooms, a large terrace of 40 sq. meters, and being near the church, it was in the same apartment complex as Leanne and Sebastien. We felt like the Lord had reserved this place for us, so did the paper-work, took out a small loan, and for the first time we became home owners after 39 years of renting!

More Renovating!

Needless to say, the apartment had to be completely redone after being empty for 7 years. So we started cleaning, sanding, painting and putting in parquet flooring. There were no kitchen cabinets, only a sink, so we went with the measurements and had a kitchen designed by computer. Bob had never put in a kitchen, so asked the guardian to help him get started, and even though he felt unsure of himself, he did a great job! Cutting out the spaces for the sink and vitro-ceramic stove make him especially uneasy! When we measured before ordering our kitchen cabinets, we had neglected to measure the space the radiator took beside the door to the terrace. As the men worked, I was praying that the cabinets would fit and leave enough space for the refrigerator. There was just enough space, praise the Lord.

We were not the only ones who had to look for a place to move into! Our son, Lance, had been living with us while he looked for work. When he got a position at Disneyland Paris, he had to commute from the NW suburbs to the SE suburbs which took one and a half to two hours. So, he found a studio near his work and got moved. We

CHAPTER 10: OUR OWN BUILDING

were able to help him out with furniture since we had more than we needed.

When the time came to pack up Bob's office in the old building, he couldn't face it psychologically, therefore a colleague's wife and I took 3-4 days going through newspapers, magazines, books, notebooks, and office supplies, putting the most essential in boxes. The garbage bin allotted for printed matter was filled to the brim and emptied several times!

The room we designated as a storage room for SS literature, flannel graph, and supplies and equipment for Awana Club, had a rickety old wooden floor that had to be removed. In its place, the men had cement poured which not only gave a certain stability, but also raised it enough so it was level with adjoining rooms. The day the truck came to pour the cement, we all donned our rubber boots and spread it as fast as we could!

Bob purchased a load of folding tables at an auction and church members donated furniture for the nursery and plants for the entry way. Our building became not only a church home for Christians, but an attractive place to find the Savior. The place which had been used for displaying coffins and tombstones became a place to find new life; eternal life! From death unto life!

Because Bob was slender, he was able to get up into the attic to put in new insulation, while the other men were too heavy. Then there were light fixtures to change and wiring for the new lights and the sound system. It seemed like every time I went over to the church, he was perched somewhere up above us all. Several of our men took time off to work on the renovations, and even some ladies did painting, varnishing, wall-papering, and cleaning. A few provided meals for the team, as it was a big job cooking for that many folks. We needed someone with knowledge and experience to install radiators and gas lines, so were very thankful when Robert and Joyce were free to come. Their ministry is to help build new churches in France, and to help others redo older buildings They also finished laying the floor tile in the fellowship hall.

Furnishings

It was wonderful to see how the Lord provided the needs of furniture as well as supplies. Roland was in the process of doing paperwork to retire from the French telephone company, which was shutting down one of their large office buildings and consolidating. He asked if they were going to take down a long row of ceiling to floor storage cabinets that covered one wall. He was told that he could have them if he came and took them all down and had them out before they emptied the rest of the building. So, we rounded up a group of our

CHAPTER 10: OUR OWN BUILDING

members, borrowed a couple of trucks, and went to dismantle them. When we got back to the church with them, we were overwhelmed to find they fit exactly on the wall we had designated. Roland also was given metal cabinets for the SS rooms, tables for our church dinners, a large safe, about 15 large metal storage cabinets that we use for stocking office supplies, children's literature and cleaning products. There was also a photocopier, a chariot for hauling cleaning needs around as one works, and many other useful and needed items, including a dishwasher, frames on wheels for trash bags, and portable fans for ventilation.

Our members also made donations such as a microwave oven, a stainless steel sink and counter top, a refrigerator, a baby bed, changing table, toys for the nursery, etc. Every need was filled either by a material or money donation.

In all, the renovation in both the front and back of the building took 5 years. The men came every Saturday they could manage to, and Bob took 2 days a week to work on the building. Finally, in the spring of 2006, we were able to have the official inauguration! Oscar borrowed slides and photos from us and others, and made a DVD of the history and beginnings of the church. We designed special invitations to send to pastors and churches in the area, plus to the mayor and other officials.

HIS HAND IN OUR LIVES

The mayor's first assistant accepted the invitation, therefore Bob asked him to say a few words.

He congratulated the members for their efforts and said how encouraging it was to have a group of people and families who obeyed the laws of the Land and lived peaceably.

As the service continued with other speakers, pastors, the choir and other music, our hearts were overwhelmed as we reviewed all that the Lord had done. The verse on the wall behind the pulpit fit the circumstance perfectly: We could truly say, *"The Lord hath done great things for us."* Psalm 126:3

CHAPTER 11: THE HUFFMAN HOTEL

"Use hospitality one to another without grudging." I Peter 4:9

There was one thing we did a lot of, and that was opening our home to visitors. From the start in Colombes, even before we finished language school, we received news that Butch and Margie ABBETT would be arriving to begin language studies. At the time, we had a Toyota four-passenger with a small trunk. Bob felt impressed to add a luggage rack to be sure and have enough space for suitcases and bags. When he arrived at the airport, not only were the Abbetts waiting, but another family of three going on to the Ivory Coast was waiting too. I'll never know how they all crowded into that small car, but they made it to Colombes! All eight of them! We had arranged our three-room apartment so that each family had a room, with place to sleep at least. Our son, Lance, was only two months old and the Skelton's baby, one month old. They didn't have a bed for Jason, so we unhooked the top part of our very European baby carriage and got him settled in.

After getting over jet lag, the two couples began looking for apartments, preferably furnished. Since there were few furnished apartments, we helped them find some furniture and appliances—used but in good shape—just enough to get started. So, two weeks after arriving, the Abbetts got moved, and the Skeltons a few days later.

The three men got together weekly to pray, and we celebrated the holidays together, so our children became like cousins. All too soon, each family moved away, to begin a work in the place the Lord had directed them to. After the Skeltons left for Africa, we still got together with the Abbetts for the holidays.

Child Evangelism Team

During the first summer after we moved to the ZUP we had a team with us for a week from CEF. Wendy stayed on with us for several months doing children's Bible Clubs.... (see chapter on children's work) By then we had more room, so our visitors were more comfortable. The next guests were René and Rosaria Durand and their two small sons. They had learned from mutual friends that we lived in Argenteuil. Since that was where René grew up, his parents lived there still, and they wanted to visit with them. Their apartment only had two rooms so we invited them to stay with us. Thus, we

CHAPTER 11: THE HUFFMAN HOTEL

got to know them and have followed their ministry in Italy through the years.

A few months later René was in the area, this time by himself, so spent the night with us. He was especially touched by the state of the homeless since he had been one of them before he found Christ. One day he witnessed to a young man without a job, home, or family. Since he had no other place to go, René brought him to our apartment where he had a meal, a bath, had his clothes washed and dried, and got a good night's sleep. He left in the morning, so I went to get his sheets and wash them. René informed me that the young man had tuberculosis. At first, I was afraid; putting a family with three little ones in jeopardy was scary! Then, as I thought about it, I realized that all this was in the Lord's hands, and that he would protect us as He promised in His Word because we are His children! So, I put the sheets, pillowcase and towels on the highest temperature (in Europe the washers heat the water) and trusted God to make sure all the germs were washed away!

More Missionaries To Africa

Another family, Jon and Carolyn De Rusha, was on their way to Africa and needed to learn French. Since we had moved a month earlier, we kept the apartment in Colombes for them as it was convenient for commuting to Paris for the Alliance française. They had three children and a fourth on the way, therefore they needed more space. When they saw the three rooms we had lived in, it was too much emotionally for Carolyn, so we let the apartment go and they began looking for a larger place. They spent six weeks with us until they found an apartment and purchased enough furniture to move in. The whole time they were with us, there was never any friction in spite of being overcrowded with ten people, six of them children. They never even complained about the simple but nourishing and inexpensive meals I prepared except once when I made a big pot of split-pea soup. Jon didn't care for that, so he teased me for days. I often sent him a package of dried split pea soup. In Africa, it probably tasted pretty good!

Cooking for a crowd

CHAPTER 11: THE HUFFMAN HOTEL

Since we had begun having regular meetings in our fourth-floor apartment, I had to pay special attention to keeping the house picked up and clean. I've always thanked the Lord for such a meticulous husband, for because of that he helped me often by vacuuming, mopping, and even washing dishes. In addition to children's clubs, we began a Bible study on Wednesday evenings for adults, and services on Sunday morning. As the group expanded, a larger place was desperately needed, and the Lord gave us a house just a few minutes away.

A Larger Place

The summer after our move, Tom and his sister, Linda Butz, came for six weeks and were a great help and encouragement to us. Tom did some painting, put up a ceiling in the chapel, and varnished 20-30 folding chairs, while his sister Linda typed up a series of correspondence courses in French, helped with preparing meals, and taught Lauri to read English. During their stay, a group from England on their way to Spain stopped for a night, so we had a crowd: 19 around the table. That makes for a lot of cooking plus a lot of dishes to wash and I didn't finish until 3 p.m! Tom took his turn washing dishes one day, and when I walked by the kitchen door, there was Tom on his knees washing the dishes! Our sink was unusually low, I might add, and Tom was unusually tall! Anyway, that evening as we were talking about it, I mentioned that it would really be nice to have a dishwasher. Bob kind of chuckled, and said I would have to wait until I got to heaven to get one. I replied, "Then I'm going to pray for one." About a month later after Tom and Linda went home to Indiana, we received a generous check from their father, a thoracic surgeon, with a note saying, "Tom and Linda think Mrs. Huffman needs a dishwasher." A definite and specific answer to prayer! "Is my hand shortened at all...?" (Isaiah 50:2)

Summer Missionaries

In the spring of each year we made an offer to house and feed any young person who would like to work as a summer missionary. For three successive summers, different young ladies came and helped immensely with stamping our address on tracts and distributing them, preparing illustrated songs for children's work, music, typing, cooking, sewing and helping out at camp. Not only does this help us in the ministry, but it gives them a greater understanding of the spiritual need here in France and around the world. One of them, Cathy, was especially talented in art, therefore, she did lovely art work on illustrated songs for the children's ministry. We still use them today. She was a French teacher in a Christian academy so was improving her French by translating lessons for her youth meetings. Each of these young ladies was a

CHAPTER 11: THE HUFFMAN HOTEL

blessing and a help to us and I'm sure they learned much about reaching out and sharing the Gospel.

One winter there was unrest in Chad, Africa, and many mission workers had to leave for a time. Jerry and Marguerite Pauley were among them. Because they felt the problem would be short-lived, they didn't want to go to the States. They stayed with us for about two weeks, waiting, waiting, waiting... then were able to make definite plans about their future.

Another couple that stayed in our home was Richard and Beverly Chivers, who were teachers at Bob Jones University. They were in the Paris area for advanced studies in French and had been granted an apartment in Argenteuil. Bob and I had to be away for several days, so the Chivers and their children stayed with our three so they wouldn't miss school. We enjoyed their fellowship for the year they were here.

Helpers In The Ministry

Then there was the Lindquist family on their way to Senegal that stayed over a month while searching for an apartment and furniture. They got settled right after I left for the hospital to welcome our fourth child into the family. They attended the church while in language training, then when we left for furlough, moved into our house in order to assure a presence for the meetings. It was later when we had to move out of the house that they were such a great help to us! Swant also went to summer camp with Paul Dédéyan and was the camp nurse since he had had medical training in the Green Berets. The campers called him Daktari because he "doctored the beasts."

In September 1973, upon arriving back in France after our first furlough, we were surprised to learn that a team from the south of France would arrive the next day for a week to do literature distribution. Did I ever have to scramble, getting groceries, making beds, unpacking and getting over jet lag! It was a lot all at once, and before they left we had to come to an understanding: if I did all the cooking, someone else would take care of the clean-up and washing dishes.

Parade Of Visitors

After we moved to town it seemed like there was an endless parade of visitors! One French teacher brought his class of 20 to Paris several years in a row. A couple of our supporting pastors came to see the work, Americans in the military in Germany stopped by when they came to visit Paris, and back-packers spent a night or two. A few members of the family finally got to France, also! My mother came over three times, Bob's mother came with Lauri one spring, and even Bob's brother and wife spent a couple of weeks so we traveled

CHAPTER 11: THE HUFFMAN HOTEL

together and were their translators. For folks who came to see Paris, Bob used to say he would give them either the 25 cents tour or the 50 cents tour. He would load them into the VW bus and take them to see Paris by night after the heavy traffic cleared out. During the day they went by themselves, for the train station was only three blocks away and once you understand the train/metro system in Paris, it's very easy to get around.

We also hosted the BIMI European Conference two or three times and usually ended up with someone at the house before or after. All these visitors contributed to making sure that we had an interesting and varied life, to say the least! When the conferences were held elsewhere, we were able to travel and visit other European countries, as well as meet other Christian workers. Later conferences were held in Germany, Spain, Switzerland, Wales, Republic Czech, and England.

Several family members came and spent time with us, including my aunt Eleanor and Lennie, my cousin, then later on Lennie and her husband, Bob's cousin Kay and son Billy, and Kelly, my cousin's daughter. My dad and wife, Jeanie, came for Licia's wedding which I will mention later.

Occasionally one of our supporting pastors would visit, including Guy Goodell, Collins Glenn, Randy Bell, Greg Allison, plus some of our individual supporters; the Dudeks, and Bill King. And, of course, lots of missionaries and their families profited from our "place oF rest and restoring": The Johnsons, Braggs, Bowens, Platilleros, Engleharts, Kidds, Ron White, Todds, the Amos family, Dan Truax, the Rays, the Elzeys.

Knock To Come Out

Some families called our place the Huffman Hotel because we had so many visitors, and one wife remarked "Most missionary families leave their welcome mat out because they rarely have company and would love having some visitors, but you should be about ready to pull yours in!" Keeping the old house clean was a big order with a gas station just across the street, which caused a film of black dust to settle on everything. Making up beds and washing sheets, plus extra shopping and preparing huge meals kept me very busy, but we enjoyed the fellowship so much I did not want to complain. Our children, however, sometimes had a hard time staying on a regular schedule and keeping up with their studies when the house was full of vacationers. Most of the time we arranged things so they didn't have to give up their beds because the visitors slept either in the office, living room or basement. They did, however, need to shower upstairs in the bathroom that opened into the girl's room, so sometimes there were surprises in early morning. Dr Butz, one of our special friends

CHAPTER 11: THE HUFFMAN HOTEL

who visited often, said "That's the only bathroom I know of where you have to knock to come OUT!"

Church Families

In addition to all the visitors, there was occasionally a family in the church who had problems and needed a place to stay for a few weeks or months. One family consisted of a mother and her two teenage daughters who, due to unfortunate circumstances, found themselves without lodging. When they called me, I had the car that day, so left immediately to go pick them up. They were at a bus stop surrounded by all their earthly belongings, and had nowhere else to go. Since the basement was free at the time (we met in the church building behind the house by then) we were glad to let them stay until they could find something suitable in their price range. That way they were warm and had a roof over their heads

The next day Denise came over and took the mother to city hall to sign up for an apartment subsidized by the government. I thought, "They won't have anything for months because the demand is so great." But Denise turned over every stone and somehow was able to talk the social workers into giving the family emergency shelter, which later on became permanent. So after less than a week they were assigned a three-room apartment into which they could move. It was a definite answer to prayer, for only the Lord's hand could bring about such a result! This family remained faithful to the church for many years until they were allotted a larger apartment farther away from Argenteuil. The mother still attends quite regularly depending on her health, for it takes time to ride the train and then a bus to get there.

Housing was still scarce when an African dad and four of his children found themselves with nowhere to live. The father worked full time at night and could pay rent, but there was nothing available that they could afford. Besides, many people were selective concerning to whom they rented. Bob said they could say in the basement (there was no room elsewhere) until they found something, and even though they signed up for government housing, there was none to be had. After the dad left for work in the evening, the boys would often stay up and play until one or two in the morning, and it was very disturbing with all the noise, for our bedroom was on that side of the house. The girls used our kitchen to prepare their meals, because they have their own African dishes they are used to eating, but from time to time we invited them to share a meal with us. I did have to remind the girls to clean up the kitchen when they were finished.

Finally, after seven months with us, Bob told the dad because he found nothing available in the

CHAPTER 11: THE HUFFMAN HOTEL

area that he needed to look in towns farther out from Paris so they could get settled before another school year began. He found a large house about two hours away and was able, therefore, to have his wife and youngest daughter join them. She had been waiting in Africa for 2-3 years! At last the family was reunited! The father found a better job in daylight hours, and they were very happy and prosperous in their new situation.

This Old House saw many friends come and go, and we gladly offered hospitality to each one for the 24 years that we lived there.

CHAPTER 12: THE LATER YEARS: BOB'S ILLNESS

"But know that the LORD hath set apart him that is godly for himself:..." Psalm 4:3

By early 2008, the church in Argenteuil had grown, matured, and was well established. Bob felt it was time to inform the members that he was planning to retire so they could form a committee and start searching for a new pastor. Nothing was done, so in the fall the church council took it upon themselves to contact a former member who found Christ through the ministry of the church, and ask him if he would help out for a while. He agreed, and at a special members' meeting, it was voted to call Aldo Atzori as pastor.

The new pastor and his wife

CHAPTER 12: THE LATER YEARS: BOB'S ILLNESS

During the holidays, Bob and I began putting bookshelves in the small office of our apartment, and started transferring Bob's volumes, notes and equipment out of the church office. Our desire and project was to offer our services to replace other French pastors' and missionaries for the time they needed, giving them and their families a much-needed rest. Therefore, in January 2009, in a touching ceremony consecrating Aldo as pastor and showing appreciation for our past ministry, we began making plans to visit and help one of our church's missionaries, René Durand in Italy.

But the Lord had other plans. The winter weather was so severe, not only in France but in Italy as well, that any travel plans had to be cancelled. In February, Bob complained about having digestive problems, so our general practitioner sent him to a specialist. After one test, then another, and another, a tumor was located in his pancreas. He was in great shape physically and continued jogging twice a week at the Ile Marante Park across the river. Therefore, doctors suggested that they try and remove the tumor to do a biopsy on it with hopes that it was benign.

Extensive Surgery

Our son-in-law Sebastien had a friend who worked as a surgical nurse for an excellent visceral surgeon in a reputable hospital nearby. He phoned her and she was able to set up an appointment right away so Bob could see him. He was so kind to work us into his busy schedule and gave up his day off to perform the surgery.

This was especially hard on Licia, our daughter, who is a medical doctor, to learn that the pancreas was affected. She pretty well knew what was ahead, but stayed optimistic about the coming surgery. We were informed that the operation would include removing, not only the tumor, but part of his stomach, duodenum and his gall bladder as well. It was invasive surgery which took more than 7 hours.

For two weeks he stayed in intensive care with high doses of morphine for pain. At one point the morphine caused him to have hallucinations and the hospital personnel had to restrain him forcefully when he tried to get up with the IV and other tubing still attached.

Chemotherapy

Slowly he began to heal and was transferred immediately to a room, but he only stayed a few days before the doctor allowed him to go home. Almost immediately he started chemotherapy, and after each session he had to rest a good bit. He was nauseated but didn't vomit, and in general, felt like he had a light case of the flu. I could tell when he had pain, but he rarely complained. We always

CHAPTER 12: THE LATER YEARS: BOB'S ILLNESS

went to see his doctor together, and each of us gave our version of how he felt, giving his doctor a complete picture. His appetite was not very good at first, so I decided to prepare everything fresh; no canned or prepared food at all. He liked carrot juice and a few other natural juices, so we kept a small quantity in the refrigerater after making fresh. That summer, because of special, loving care, lots of visits from members of the church, and from his children, etc. he began to feel better, giving us hope that his system was overcoming the cancer. In November we went for his check-up, and x-rays showed the tumor had not grown back. There were just a few nodules but nothing serious.

Fifteen More Years?

I was so excited about the prospect of Bob being healed that it was hard to stay calm. I went into the bedroom to pray and laid out my heart before the Lord. I remembered how King Hezekiah wept before the Lord upon learning that he was "sick unto death" and reminded God how he had "walked in truth and with a perfect heart, and have done that which is good in thy sight." And the response: "I have heard thy prayer, I have seen thy tears: behold, I will add unto thy days fifteen years." And with a broken heart and overflowing of tears, I asked God to give Bob another fifteen years also. And His answer? Just as plain as day He replied, "I already have!"

I was so shocked! I got up off my knees and sat on the bed trying to figure out what transpired fifteen years before. Then I remembered. Yes, it was the time he was very ill, so our doctor ran tests and had him admitted to the clinique, but they couldn't find any problem, even after X-rays, a sonogram and blood tests. So, they sent him home. But the symptoms persisted. He was sitting at the table and I was ironing. He tried to eat something, but was so nauseated he couldn't. He looked at me and said, "The Lord told me it would be 13 days." He was still so sick I called our doctor once again, and he came on a house call to see him. He had him readmitted to the clinique and told them to run more tests – the same ones if necessary. They did, and had several of the doctors look at them, and together they found something. However, they had little assurance of what it was nor how it developed. It was located so far back in his pelvic area that it was very difficult to see; they couldn't find it on the first tests. Even the blood tests did not show an increase in white blood cells which would indicate infection.

Emergency surgery was scheduled for the next morning. When I saw the surgeon afterwards he was shaking his head and saying he had never seen a pocket of infection so well hidden or so far back! His theory, and the other doctors agreed, was that there had been infection in his appendix and

CHAPTER 12: THE LATER YEARS: BOB'S ILLNESS

the body's reaction was to coat it and envelop it for several weeks or months instead of letting it enlarge and spread. I remembered that five months before he had gone for a colonoscopy, which showed 3-4 small polyps and one larger one in the area of the appendix. All seemed normal, but about a month later he began vomiting during the night so violently that I called "Medecins de nuit" (Doctors by night). The doctor came and gave him an injection which calmed the vomiting and he was back on his feet after a day's rest. At the time I didn't think any more about it, but a doctor friend in the US mentioned the fact that sometimes after the removal of polyps there is a tiny cut or tear in the colon which can allow leakage and cause infection. This could have been a possibility, but as I thought about this, I realized that no matter what caused it, the Lord had His hand on Bob for the time that passed before they found the infection! And I praised Him and thanked Him for His protection!

Intensive Care

Bob stayed in the clinique in intensive care for 13 days, just like the Lord had indicated to him. When he came home he was still very weak so couldn't take on a full schedule of teaching and preaching, etc. Friends opened their home on the beach in northern France for a time of recuperation, so we drove up and spent time walking on the beach among the dunes, and just reading and relaxing. We didn't learn until later from our doctor that Bob had just barely pulled through, and that all the doctors at the Clinique were having tests run to make sure they didn't have a hidden infection somewhere!

As I mulled over all these former happenings, it became clear what the Lord was telling me. If God had already given my dear husband 15 years grace to live and serve Him, then through this illness He was going to call him to his heavenly home. I couldn't cry or even be really sad, because looking towards heaven is such a joyous thought and hope! He was going to his heavenly home and even though we all wished God would leave him with us, I could only be glad for him and long to go with him. At the time my task was to help him get through this illness and the multiplied treatments!

The holiday season was coming up, and of course, we were busy with preparations for the Christmas program at church, as well as getting together as a family. Since Bob was feeling better, he signed up to do the cleaning at the church one week late in December. When he returned to our apartment, he was exhausted and had a severe backache. He took some Tylenol and rested a while, but told me, "The cancer is returning; I can feel it in my back." At his next doctors' visit, tests showed he was correct, so they started another round of

CHAPTER 12: THE LATER YEARS: BOB'S ILLNESS

chemotherapy which was more potent. It was to last 6 months.

The Cancer Returns

Bob began enumerating the things he would like to do before going to be with the Lord. He knew, and now I knew, that his time was limited, therefore he wanted to make the best of it while he could still get around. One of his greatest desires was to see his family in the US. That meant asking his doctors if they would recommend that he travel. They gave him permission as long as he continued the treatment while away. We contacted a good friend who was a nurse in Chattanooga, and she put us in touch with a Christian doctor who was experienced in the kind of treatment Bob needed. We worked out a schedule that allowed us to be in the Chattanooga area when he needed the chemotherapy, then started looking into prices for direct flights from Paris to Atlanta-Chattanooga. When we got the trip all lined up, he seemed relieved knowing he would see them all one last time.

Another thing he wanted to do was go on a cruise. I contacted Bill and Peggy and asked them about it since they had been on cruises before, and they began looking for a cruise with room for four; not too expensive and not too long. They found one that took 3 – 4 days going around to the different large towns and islands in the Gulf of Mexico for a reasonable price. So we signed up for that, and tried to keep him well so he wouldn't be sick on the boat.

The time spent in the States was enjoyable for Bob. Our daughter Lauri had reserved a furnished apartment at the next-door neighbors' so he was able to rest when he needed to and especially after each session of chemotherapy. When he felt better he was able to get out to visit friends, and for his 72nd birthday we planned a quiet surprise party with several old friends coming over. Not only was he surprised, he was especially pleased that everyone would think of him that day.

40 Years of Service

Another pleasant surprise was planned by the directors at the Mission office in Harrison, TN. The men realized that, because we had been on the field so much and when we did get to the US we didn't stay long, that Bob had never received a pin for 25 years of faithful service, after we had been serving in France for 40 years plus! They called our family and friends and held a short but touching ceremony which included testimonies of his faithfulness before presenting him with a plaque with congratulations for 40 years of service in the Lord's work.

CHAPTER 12: THE LATER YEARS: BOB'S ILLNESS

Final Decision

Our stay in the US was satisfying and everything turned out well for Bob. Upon returning to our home in France he had an appointment for X-rays and other tests to see if the second series of chemo had been effective. The tests showed that nothing had changed for the better; the cancer was spreading. The doctors prescribed a third series of chemotherapy which was much stronger than the first two, and said it would give him an upset stomach and diarrhea and be very difficult to take. Bob asked for a few days before he gave his answer. A couple evenings later, Leanne and Sebastien came over to talk. Bob told them and me at the same time what he had decided; what he felt the Lord would have him do. He knew deep down that the Lord was going to take him home, so it would be of no value to continue treatments and suffer, besides making his family suffer as well. It was a hard decision to make and hard for us to find out. So we surrounded him with as much love and care as we could!

In the meantime, Leanne had some dear friends from their church who had moved to Lyon, France, and had a large house with swimming pool and a nice yard. They were going away on vacation for a couple of weeks, and when they found out about Bob's illness, they offered to let whole family stay there for a restful vacation. It was just what he needed; to spend time with his family in a quiet area which also allowed the children to enjoy youthful activities. Sebastien would drive us down, which was very kind. The girls arranged our bedroom with an adjustable lounge chair for Bob to sleep in, which for him was more comfortable than a bed.

Family Vacation

We spent a very happy and satisfying time there, and Bob was completely relaxed. He had no demands to fulfill, so he just rested and read, watched a little TV and spent time with his grandchildren.

Sebastien had put together a DVD that told of Bob's life with photos incorporated and it was fitting for the time and for the person it honored. I would like to view it once again, but haven't dared because I know I will cry a river. It's something the future members of the family might enjoy and learn from. Not having known him when joining our family leaves an enormous void.

Upon returning to our apartment in Argenteuil, it was time to make preparation for the future while Bob could still get around. We went to the bank and arranged things so I could have the finances for burial expenses. We sold our nice Toyota van to one of the men in the church so he could use it for people he invited for church. Even though I could drive it with no problem, working the

CHAPTER 12: THE LATER YEARS: BOB'S ILLNESS

clutch made my left leg very painful. Bob thought a used automatic would be easier for me to drive. In France there aren't too many automatics, but eventually we found a Ford focus in excellent shape. It was just what I needed and we thanked the Lord for leading us to the right place! His hand was always there to show us the way!

Right across the street from the entry to the hospital there was a small funeral home, so I made an appointment to see the personnel there. By that time Bob was too tired to go with me. It had no parking area and walking would have been too tiring for Bob. They helped me work out the financial aspects of the funeral and took care of going to city hall to reserve a plot in the cemetery. They took care of all the details, for which I was thankful, and even came by the apartment to discuss the plan, and find out if Bob had any special desires for the funeral or the burial.

Palliative Care

As his health declined, we knew the next step was to sign up for palliative care (like hospice) at the hospital, which was just a block away. They were in the process of adding a wing for palliative care so didn't have offices for consultations as yet. Therefore, when I called to make an appointment, one of the doctors and a nurse walked over to see the state of Bob's illness. From then on they made house calls, which made it easier for everyone, especially Bob.

A few weeks into the fall, he had to be hospitalized after he fell getting up from a chair and hit his head on a radiator. He was the first patient in the new wing. For a few days he was subject to confusion, but this cleared up with no problem. Licia came often from Lille in Northern France, and because she is a doctor working in palliative care, she was able to help out a great deal. Often she would call the director of the wing and they would discuss Bob's case. It was comforting to me to have her there when she could come!

Bob's brother Bill and his wife Peggy came over to spend time with Bob and stayed a month. They helped out so much and I really appreciated their presence. Mickey and Cookie Johnson came from Germany and stayed a couple of days encouraging Bob and comforting me. Rod and Lindy Kidd also came from Germany and stayed in a bed and breakfast in Argenteuil that we didn't know existed. And others from around Paris stopped by including Paul and Alexis Dedeyan, Andrew Barnes, most all of the members of the church, plus quite a few of our neighbors. The nurses were amazed at the number of visitors that came! Bob was an easy patient to care for, and rarely called or interrupted their rounds They were thankful because he would be spending several more weeks at the hospital.

CHAPTER 12: THE LATER YEARS: BOB'S ILLNESS

The Last Letter to our Supporters

Dear Pastors, intercessors, supporting churches and special friends,

There are some among you who have prayed for us and sent support from the beginning of our ministry in 1969. Others have joined along the way. We love and respect each one of you because of your consecration and faithfulness to the great commission. You were there when we had physical and physical needs! You were with us when two young Christians with two little girls only 2 and 6 left all they knew to go to a foreign country, language and culture. You stayed with us as we labored to learn French, trying at the same time to make contacts and share the love of Christ with them.

We were aware of your prayers as we witnessed to neighbors, fellow students, and later to merchants in the open market where we held a Bible and book stand. You went with us through each step of the ministry, from starting with English classes and Bible clubs in the high-rise apartment complex, to the house where we held services in the garage turned chapel, to the old stone house in town where we met first in the living-dining room, then in the basement, and finally in a renovated workshop just behind the house.

You accompanied us through each phase of outreach: the recorded telephone messages, tract distribution, summer and winter camps, the ladies meetings, the youth group, Awana clubs, films, concerts and the radio program the church sponsored.

You stayed by us as the children grew up; through our son Lance's meningitis, our daughter Lauri's bout with Hodgkin's disease; and now through my wife's Parkinson's Disease.

You were faithful to pray and give as the church outgrew the building and as we searched for a place to purchase in 2000-2001. You saw God answer prayer and give us our present building and you stayed with us through the years of renovation and for the inauguration.

Now the church has called a national pastor and the ministry and outreach goes on through the Christians we have trained to take over the teaching and other responsibilities. The Lord has been so good to us and we praise His Name. Just last Sunday the youth leader shared that seven teens made professions of faith at a dinner and meeting on Saturday night! As the Christians continue to reach out, we have been made even more aware of the need by the fact that the largest mosque in Europe is only 4 blocks away from our church. It was inaugurated last Friday with many important government officials present for the ceremony, as well as TV cameras, etc. Please remember the spiritual needs of Argenteuil in your prayers.

As most of you know, my physical status has been affected by pancreatic cancer, and tests

CHAPTER 12: THE LATER YEARS: BOB'S ILLNESS

show that the chemotherapy has not had the desired effect. Therefore all treatments have been stopped and we don't know what the future holds. Of one thing we are sure: we know the Lord holds the future in His Hands, and we are trusting Him completely for the outcome.

"As for me, behold, I am in your hand: do with me as seemeth good and meet unto you." Jer. 26:14

Until He Comes,
Bob and Gail Huffman

CHAPTER 13: HIS LAST DAYS

"For God is not unrighteous to forget your work and labour of love, which ye have shewed toward his name..." Hebrews 6:10

As Bob's illness progressed, the medication no longer relieved the pain, even when increased. The doctor had allowed him to spend time at home at the end of October, and he was able to be there when Bill and Peggy left to return to Tampa, Florida. But his stay was short-lived because he was in pain, and the doctor re-admitted him. When the ambulance drivers came to get him and take him down the stairs in a chair, I went down to the entry hall to see him go. I couldn't help but think, "That was the last time for him to be at home." I knew he didn't have long to live, so I called our oldest daughter in TN and told her it was time for her to come. I really needed some help as well as comfort with all the visitors and just everyday tasks because of spending so much time at the hospital. And she wanted to be with her dad while they could still have time together.

Bob was especially glad to see Lauri, and in the evenings after supper she would go and stay

CHAPTER 13: HIS LAST DAYS

with her dad for a couple of hours. He asked me one day to have all four of our children come to his bedside that week so that he could talk to them. On the special evening we brought in extra chairs and sat around his bed. He shared his thoughts with us, and thanked the Lord that his children all knew and followed the Lord, and he shared his desire that they always remain faithful to our heavenly Father. He also asked them to take care of their mother who had Parkinson's disease. Then we sang some of his favorite hymns softly so as not to disturb others. Even so our voices could be heard and the nurses and other personnel would come by and have a look at what was going on.

On Her Knees

Bob's testimony was known and shared among the hospital personnel because it was so unusual to see a patient accept the fact that his life would soon be snuffed out. He still had a burning desire to share the Gospel and see someone come to know the Lord. He talked to each of his caretakers about his or her soul, and each one had a great respect for God's Word. They didn't mock or make fun of it like so many did. One time I was with him in the afternoon and a blonde nurse came in to check his blood pressure. Bob began talking to her about eternity, and because his voice was weak, she had difficulty hearing him. So she got down on her knees to listen closely until the end of the conversation.

We invited many of the doctors and nurses to the church, and after Bob passed away, I prepared a packet of tracts and left them at the nurses' station along with a very large basket of fresh fruit. From time to time when I was at the hospital for a rendezvous, I would go by and thank them again for all they had done for Bob.

In The Morning

The last week in November the temperature dropped and we had freezing weather and snow for several days. On Sunday afternoon I had gone to the hospital to spend time with Bob and encourage him. He was sound asleep and didn't stir when I talked to him. I could tell the end was near and that old Gospel hymn came to mind, "I'll see you in the morning" and "the morning" was in heaven. So I softly sang it, and walked home, filled with sadness because of his suffering but rejoicing that he would soon be with his precious Lord whom he had served so faithfully.

When the phone rang the next morning at about 6:30, I knew who it was. The hospital was calling to tell us Bob Huffman was with the Lord. Lauri knew also who it was, so we dressed quickly and walked over, through the falling snow on slippery streets. The white flakes seemed so

CHAPTER 13: HIS LAST DAYS

appropriate at the time, reminding us of Christ's sinless life and the pardon He offered. "Whiter than snow" was the song that came to mind, and the snow also made me think of Bob's life since finding the Savior. It was not sinless, but so pure compared the world and the desires of most human hearts.

Into His Arms

Upon arriving at the hospital one of the nurses who took care of Bob was just leaving, so she stopped and related his last hours and minutes before going to meet his Savior. He had been calm most of the night and just sweetly slipped away into the waiting arms of his heavenly Father.

When we got to his room, we sat praying for a few minutes because we felt we were on holy ground. Then we gathered up his things and called the other children. Leanne came right to the hospital and went to his room but it was a much too emotional moment for her to bear. Later that morning we walked over to the funeral home to make last minute plans, and upon returning home I began addressing the cards to all our friends and neighbors telling of his home-going and time of the funeral. The funeral home had printed these cards and all that remained to do was put down the day and time of the ceremony at the church.

HIS HAND IN OUR LIVES

I was thankful to have this to take care of, for it kept me busy and helped me not to think of the near future without the love of my life. In addition to the cards we mailed, we tacked up notices in all the entryways of our apartment building as he was well-known in the neighborhood. From Monday to Friday, the day of the funeral, there was just enough time to let everyone know. The personnel at the Post Office always make sure these cards are classified as urgent, so they were received in a day of two.

Despite the number of cards sent out, (about 150) I was surprised at how many people attended the funeral. The church, which could seat about 200, was filled to overflowing, with folks standing in the hallways both on the side and in the back. Since the nursery had speakers, a group of folks listened in there, as well. Our four children, with the help of Pascal, had organized the order of service and the music, asking Licia to represent them and give a short talk about what he meant to them. Jocelyn and Sébastien had designed and printed attractive programs. We had never seen such a crowd! Even the men from the funeral home said this was very unusual. But I knew why there was a good turn-out; it was because we had prayed for months that Bob's home-going would be a great testimony for the Lord, and that many who had not heard would

CHAPTER 13: HIS LAST DAYS

receive the Gospel and come to the Savior. I was overwhelmed; so many lost and so few saved!

Steve Barnes presided over the ceremony and shared how he and Bob had worked together so many years in the pastoral (a group of pastors in the area who met once a month to pray together and plan special meetings for the young adults) and for the Bible Conference each spring. It was not only a time of sorrow for all who knew Bob, but also a time of rejoicing at what had been accomplished in lives and hearts that were changed by the Christ, as well as the fact that he was no longer suffering and we would be reunited one day.

Finished My Course

During the service, I could not help but think how the Lord had answered our long and earnest prayers for a permanent meeting place for our group of Christians. Now Bob's work was done, and we were honoring him for his dedication to the Lord and his love for the people of Argenteuil and surrounding towns. Here he was, in the midst of his people, in the building God had so graciously provided. Bob could say with Paul, *"I have fought a good fight, I have finished my course, I have kept the faith: Henceforth there is laid up for me a crown of righteousness, which the Lord, the righteous judge, shall give me at that day: and not to me only but to all them also that love His appearing." II Timothy 4:7,8.*

After the ceremony, the family stood in the back to greet our guests as they departed. Many took time to sign the register, which provided a list of those to whom I needed to send thank you notes. I was so excited to see certain ones I had not seen for years, that I asked them how they were. My daughter had to remind me that they wanted to express their sympathy to the family.

Last Words

The cold weather and the snow was still with us, and the funeral home was hurrying us to get to the cemetery before the daylight was gone in order to close up the grave and finish everything up. So I climbed into my son's car, and even though we went straight to the cemetery, we were holding things up for the workers because the graveside ceremony would not start until his family arrived. After the meditation was pronounced, we were given rose petals to let float down on the coffin. As the shadows crept upon us, soft snowflakes began to fall. The quiet atmosphere brought a hush over the crowd as the last words of love and respect for our pastor, friend, father and husband were pronounced, and we sang softly as we left the graveside. Robert Huffman had gone home to be with the Lord he had loved and served so faithfully.

CHAPTER 14: BOB HUFFMAN, A MAN OF CHARACTER!

"... The Lord hath set apart him that is godly for himself." Ps. 4:3.

A family man with two of our grandchildren

If ever there was a man who had principles, it was Bob Huffman. His strong points were truthfulness, honesty, punctuality, faithfulness, total commitment, and stick-to-itiveness, among others. In addition, he was thorough, organized, clean and neat.

Many times he reprimanded me for exaggerating. To him it was the same as lying; consequently, I learned to be less flowery in my descriptions. He mentioned often to his children what his mother had told him: "If you tell me one lie I'll never believe you again!" And in our 49 years of marriage, I never heard him tell an untruth or even exaggerate.

He was just as honest as he was truthful. Not only with his family, friends, and entourage, but especially with his Lord and Savior! Before he was saved, he began giving his tithe, and afterwards even more so. He gave the tithe to the church on everything we earned, and God blessed him and prospered him as He has promised. We always had what we needed, although not much extra at times.

A Paper Clip

One particular incident showed how important it was to him to be above-board in even the smallest dealings. In order to pay our electric bill in Argenteuil, we would go to the electric company's office in town to pay with a check attached by a paper clip to the part of the bill we had received in the mail. At the cashiers' window there was a small bowl of paper clips on the counter for those who needed one. As he stood there waiting for the girl

CHAPTER 13: HIS LAST DAYS

to register the payment, he picked up a paper clip and put it in his pocket. On the way out he suddenly realized: "I don't need that paper clip; I took it without asking and that's stealing!" He was so convicted he turned around and went back, put the paper clip in the bowl then left again, with a much springier step. He used this incident to illustrate the importance of honesty in one of his messages to the church and the way he told it was so touching! It impressed everyone; in fact, they still talk about it!

"If you are on time you are late," was the saying of our assistant pastor in Chattanooga. It was imperative to arrive early to be sure all was ready, to allow for unexpected developments and to have time to fellowship a minute and greet people. Bob was just as punctual in his personal life and with his family as he was in his professional life.

Bob was not an expert in mechanics, repairing electrical appliances, carpentry or redecorating, but whatever he tried to do, he thought it out thoroughly, measured, made sure he had the necessary tools, and purchased necessary materials. Then, and only then, would he tackle the job. By that time he knew pretty well what the outcome would be, and his repair work was always well done. He took the time to do it right and often said to me when I tried to take shortcuts, "If you're going to do something, do it right!" He tried to teach our children to do the same.

Line Them Up Right

In addition to that, he was exceptionally organized and neat. Over his workbench he had put a sign: "A place for everything and everything in its place." In this way he hoped to find things as he had left them, as well as to encourage our offspring to be responsible for the tools, etc. that they borrowed. If you ever opened his closet (wardrobe) you would see very neat piles of T-shirts, socks, etc. on the shelves and his dress shirts hung according to their color. One of his habits speaks loudly concerning his penchant for neatness and orderliness; every Saturday evening after the youth group, choir practice and other meetings, he would go into the church, stand behind the pulpit, and look at how the chairs were lined up, then go and straighten any that were out of line. To every member that came to clean, he would explain how to make straight lines by measuring with their feet to get the right distance between the rows. Finally, one day he made marks on the baseboards the correct distant apart, and when one of the faithful ladies cleaned the church, she laughed and laughed upon seeing the marks.

Another strong point in his character was total commitment. The Lord had called him to win

CHAPTER 13: HIS LAST DAYS

souls and establish a church, and everything he did was in relation to that calling. The varied means of getting the Gospel out that he used were mentioned on previous pages. In addition, he maintained contact with several other pastors and missionaries, and often asked what seemed to be most effective in reaching those who may be searching. He initiated the Friday evening prayer time, and when he prayed, one could feel the love he had for his Lord and for the unsaved, as well as for his brothers and sisters in Christ. Whenever someone new stopped by the church to talk, his first concern was for their soul. Therefore, he would ask, "Are you a Christian?" If they answered "Yes," he would continue, "And what did you do to become a Christian?" Many times they would answer, "Oh I was baptized in the Catholic Church as an infant," or "I took my first communion at age 12." Then he would explain that each person had to make his own personal decisions as to whether he wanted to follow Christ, adding: "God doesn't have any grandchildren." For many, this was the first time they had heard the pure Gospel, and they often gave their hearts and lives to Christ. I couldn't begin to name those that came to know Him after hearing the Gospel presented so clearly and simply.

Finally, the attribute of character that most remember him for is faithfulness. Not only did he encourage his flock to be faithful to the Lord and the church, he practiced what he preached. One of his most used phrases was, "Be faithful, young folks." He rarely accepted invitations to speak in other churches, and when he did was anxious to get home to see how things were going. He definitely had a pastor's heart and was well-loved by his brothers and sisters in Christ. He called the young ladies "his girls" and was very protective of them. One of them called him "mon petit papa" because for years he went by and picked her up for Awana Club. In fact, when she asked to be baptized, she came to me to request that Bob baptize her, but by that time he was so ill with the cancer that he couldn't even get out of bed. When I told her, tears rolled down her cheeks. Everyone felt a great loss when he was gone.

Never Give Up

Bob Huffman stuck to the task until it was accomplished, a character trait that impressed us all. One day, Terry Arp, who worked with us after leaving Africa, came by the house with a cartoon he had enlarged. On it one could see a pelican trying to swallow a frog he had caught, but the frog was strangling the pelican so that he couldn't swallow him. The caption at the bottom of the page indicated "NEVER GIVE UP!" And he didn't! It took almost 40 years to get the church well enough established so a national pastor could take over. Not only did it take many hours per week of

CHAPTER 13: HIS LAST DAYS

evangelization, of study to prepare messages and lessons, of counseling with the unsaved or with members who had problems, but there was the administrative side, because any meetings open to the public have to be registered with the county seat, and minutes have to be typed up and sent in. Most of the members understood and helped out when and where they could. There was only one member who was often in disagreement with the manner Bob handled certain things pertaining to the Church. When we had the annual business meetings, he often opposed any decisions made. One day he was murmuring and complaining about something, and Bob kindly said, "It doesn't bother me to pull the wagon by myself, but it is very difficult to pull when someone drags their feet behind it!" The murmuring subsided – for a while. I don't know if that man ever realized the effect his complaining had on other Christians.

CHAPTER 15: THE HUFFMAN KIDS

"Lo, children are an heritage of the LORD..."
Psalm 127:3

Being far away from our families in the US left an empty spot for our children, for they didn't often spend time with their grandparents, cousins, uncles and aunts, etc. Of course they wrote, and sometimes called, which helped a bit. We, as parents, tried to not only be sure they were familiar with our relatives, but showed photos and told funny incidents about them. When each child's birthday came around, we made special efforts to celebrate, preparing a special meal chosen by the child, as well as his favorite birthday cake. When they were older, it was hard to find time to do things together as a family due to their school schedules and other activities, therefore, since they didn't have classes on Wednesday afternoon, I would take one of them to shop, to eat at our favorite creperie, or do something special that they would enjoy. So once a month they had a special day with Mom.

For our family devotions we had found two books with meditations at their level, and used

CHAPTER 15: THE HUFFMAN KIDS

them for a long time. Their thinking was stimulated, and they heard English every day this way. Later on they took turns reading a passage out loud from a Bible for children. It was important to teach them spiritual truths with language they could understand, as well as increase their English vocabulary.

Each child had a different personality, therefore, instead of a homogenous group, the four of them were complete individuals. Each one was like an only child, and it took some adjusting to fill their needs.

The Huffman kids, ages 3, 8, 11, and 15

Lauri

Lauri was our firstborn, and because she was the first girl born into the Huffman family, her paternal grandmother thought she was the greatest. She enjoyed buying girlie things for her, and nick-named her Dolly, from the film and song, "Hello Dolly." She was an obedient child, sociable and content. While we studied at the University she spent her mornings in the nursery provided for the married students with families. She developed normally except for talking, and she was ahead of the normal age in language. Each word was pronounced carefully with precision, and this was to her advantage when we arrived in France.

At age 5 she attended kindergarten for a year at a nearby church. While we were on deputation she traveled with no trouble, going from place to place and making acquaintance easily. Upon arriving in France at age 6 in March, she readily made friends with the neighborhood children and played with them outside on our dead-end street. After Easter, we registered her for school and they put her in 1st grade even though she didn't speak French. During the summer, we enrolled her in the program offered by the school, so she went swimming, took long walks, played games, etc. all in total immersion in the French language. By September she was fluent and had no trouble starting first grade.

CHAPTER 15: THE HUFFMAN KIDS

Every day she brought her reading books home and we went over the vocabulary and pronunciation. It was good for Bob and me to see the vowel combinations and learn the pronunciation and phonetics. Reading with her helped us in our language study.

As she grew up, she remained a calm and serene child, even through the moves and changes in our family life. As a tiny girl, she was very interested in animals, and for many years, wanted to become a veterinarian. When she was in Junior High, she came home one day with a young magpie that had evidently fallen out of the nest. A classmate had found it and couldn't take care of it. So we put it in a cardboard box and fed it by poking pieces of scrambled egg and bread soaked in milk down his throat. He lived and grew, so we named him Maggie (we found out later he was a male). Bob built a cage in the back yard and Maggie stayed with us for a couple of years. We eventually had to give him away because he would go to the neighbors, go in through the window and make messes in their bedroom.

Throughout her schooling she was a good student; steady and regular, even though she had to study harder in high school. The French school system is not set up to encourage students and make them feel worthy. Instead, no matter how hard you work, they often say "You could do better." She began to feel she was not good enough, and this plagued her for many years.

In high school, evolution was taught not as a theory, but as truth. We have always discussed such subjects with our children, trying to show them that they need to go to God's Word to see the other side of the coin, especially since evolution has never been proved. No "missing links" have ever been found, and there have so many hoax (es) that is difficult to have faith in some scientists. Lauri knew all this, so when the day came for the test on evolution in science class, she answered every question exactly as the teacher had taught, then added her opinion at the end, sharing what the Bible says about creation with her professor. When her test paper was returned, she had an excellent grade, and the professor put at the end how impressed she was by someone who was not afraid to stand up for her beliefs. Bob and I were reassured and very proud of Lauri's courage and stand for what she believed.

Lauri had a sweet nature which seemed to attract young men. One day not long after we had moved to "this old house," a young man from the youth group knocked on the front door and asked for Lauri. She went, talked to him for a few minutes, then returned to her room. A short while later that same day, someone knocked on the back door, which I opened, and another young man

CHAPTER 15: THE HUFFMAN KIDS

asked for Lauri. Swanté Lindquist, who was with us until he left for Africa, had heard the conversations, so he slipped behind the door to the basement and closed it. Then we heard a knock, knock, knock, and when I opened the door, Swante asked timidly, "Is Lauri here?" teasing her. It seemed she had several admirers! Once we even received a letter from an African who had seen our family photo somehow and asked for Lauri's hand. We were thankful that he didn't show up on our doorstep!

In her last year of high school, she became friends with L. He was a young man in her class, one of the best-looking French boys I had ever seen. He came to the house several times and then we received an invitation to a special meal at his home. We met his parents and sisters, and enjoyed a delicious French dinner. As we got to know the family, we began to understand that the parents considered the relationship to be serious, even though they had not as yet finished high school. We knew that Lauri would be going to the US for further education, and were thinking of a long-distance relationship. We encouraged Lauri to share the testimony of her faith with him, and we talked with him also, but he wanted nothing to do with a personal relationship with the Lord, and refused categorically to consider it.

The rest of that school year was dedicated to reviewing for and taking the tests for the baccalaureate, which consists of 4-hour exams in each subject plus oral exams in each foreign language. Lauri was scheduled to fly to the US with her dad (I left earlier with the three younger children) soon after receiving the results of her tests. The evening before her departure, L. came by the house and began knocking on the metal gate outside. Young love is so irrational! He knew deep down that she might never come back, and could not deal with it emotionally. It was a difficult situation for both of them, as well as for Bob who had to deal with it, trying not to leave deep psychological scars.

At first after Lauri arrived in the US, they wrote to each other, but then L. ceased to answer. Lauri found out later that he had another girlfriend already and that he had not made the effort to let her know. Lauri was deeply hurt and felt betrayed. She had been faithful and felt he should have let her know about the change in his feelings toward her. In her heart she knew, however, that the hand of the Lord had protected her from an unequal relationship and that He had someone special that knew and loved the Lord reserved for her.

A New Country

Lauri's high school years came to an end in 1981 when she passed her tests to receive her baccalaureate from the French school systems.

CHAPTER 15: THE HUFFMAN KIDS

Since she didn't really know what she wanted to do or what she wished to study, we suggested she go to the US and begin her studies at Tennessee Temple – our alma mater – where we knew she would be secure and be under the influence and teachings of dedicated Christians who cared. That summer we were scheduled for a short furlough, so she moved into the dorm early when we got ready to return to France. All of us face difficult moments in life, and that was one of the hardest for me! Leaving my firstborn in a "foreign country" (for it was foreign to her) just tore my heart out, and as we got in the car and started the long drive from TN to FL where Bob's folks lived, I couldn't stop crying! Bob and the kids were sniffing, too, and finally Bob said, "Do you want to go back and get her?" We knew we couldn't as she had no plane ticket to France, her trunk and suitcases wouldn't fit in the car, and she was registered for classes which began in a week. So I said, "No" and we drove on, knowing we were doing the Lord's will with broken hearts!

It wasn't easy for Lauri, either, since she had grown up in France and was not acquainted with all the American customs, many of which had changed over the years. She did know English, however, and quickly learned the other habits, foods, and new vocabulary. Bob had opened a bank account for her, and she didn't know how to balance it out.

HIS HAND IN OUR LIVES

Praise the Lord, her dorm mother was willing to help her with that and other things that were so new to her. In the dorm at times there was jealousy and other problems, so with 4 girls all wanting things to go their way, at times there was friction. Lauri learned to be a peace-maker as time went on.

She decided to major in Art and enjoyed her classes where she could be creative. She tried making friends, but only felt really comfortable with missionary kids or young people from other countries, and went often to the Foreign Mission Fellowships to pray with them. Every week I wrote her a long letter, and we called her as often as we could afford to. She applied for and received a grant so that with what we sent every month she did not have to work. In the spring she found that, with the grant, she would have some money left over, so decided to use it to purchase a plane ticket to France. We were so happy to have her back for the summer!

Undetected Problem

Bob and I were going to be teaching at camp for three weeks, so she decided to go with us and help in the kitchen. All three of us needed chest X-rays, which was routine, but when we went to pick them up the doctor informed us that it looked like there was an aneurism between her heart and lungs and to see a doctor right away. Since she had a

CHAPTER 15: THE HUFFMAN KIDS

return ticket to the US, we thought it best to have her examined at the American hospital in case she needed a treatment or medication that could be continued in the US. After running tests, the doctor at the American Hospital said that no, it wasn't an aneurism, but to be sure, told us to go to the cardiology clinic to have her heart and circulatory system checked out. Everything was fine there, so they sent her by ambulance to another hospital (Saint-Louis) to see a specialist. It was there that she was diagnosed as having Hodgkin's disease with a large tumor that would have to be surgically removed. A Professor Andrieu told Lauri to go on to camp which was in July, relax and enjoy herself, and scheduled the surgery for August.

The tumor revealed the suspected Hodgkins was the culprit and its size was larger than an apricot. They had opened her thoracic cage starting from her side under her left arm all the way up to the middle of her back in order to extract the tumor, putting in 51 stitches when they sewed her up. When I went in to sit with her after the surgery that morning, I was horrified to see the extent of the scar. She was hospitalized for only 4-5 days, then came home and began chemotherapy after the scar was healed. I told Bob to take plastic bags in case she needed to throw up on the way home, and sure enough, she did. The drive to the Hospital in Paris was long and slow because of traffic but we

HIS HAND IN OUR LIVES

were thankful she didn't have to ride the train and metro! The chemo was difficult to take, and the side effects as well. Michèle A. cut her hair so the weight wouldn't make it all fall out, and she didn't feel much like eating most days.

The chemo treatments lasted for 3 months followed by a month of rest, which coincided with the Christmas holidays. It was nice to be all together once again for the holidays, even though she didn't feel very good at times.

The cobalt treatments began next. She had to go 5 days a week for these. To facilitate the task of staying within certain boundaries, small tattoo dots outlined the area to be bombarded. Her ovaries were protected by lead plates so she would not become sterile, but her esophagus became very sore and sensitive. A special diet was prescribed and followed, which included soft foods such as applesauce since she had difficulty swallowing. During all these months, she kept up part of her studies by correspondence so she wouldn't lose a whole year. To keep her mind and body active, she took First Aid classes at the fire station, and jogged with her dad to keep up her strength.

The Lord's hand was seen in all these events, first because the Hodgkin's was discovered while she was home with her family, surrounded with care and love; secondly, one of the best centers in the world for treating Hodgkin's is in Paris, France.

CHAPTER 15: THE HUFFMAN KIDS

Third, it was found in its early stages, therefore responded well to treatment and, fourth, her plane ticket had an open return date, so she could use it when she was ready.

As the end of the treatments came around, Lauri decided, after much prayer and discussion, to return to TTU and finish her studies. We had told her she could stay in France and study if she preferred, and we would renovate the basement so she could have her own little studio. But she chose to return to Tampa, FL in late spring to spend a few weeks resting and regaining her strength before going back to the University. For ten years following her illness, she had to get a check-up and physical exam every 6 months to be sure the Hodgkin's did not return, and praise the Lord, she has been cancer-free for over 30 years! We are forever thankful to God for sparing our Lauri.

Licia

Our second daughter, Licia was born four years after Lauri. My mother, who lived in Chattanooga at the time, teased me about having the baby on April first. That was definitely not to my liking, so I responded, "I don't want an April Fool baby! It won't come today, I won't let it!" And I didn't. The next morning was Sunday. I began having contractions but didn't want to stay at home alone while Bob and Lauri went to Sunday school and church and not have a way to get to the hospital if needed. Therefore, I packed my bag and went along, making arrangements for friends to pick Lauri up after Sunday school if we weren't there. During the Bible study, I timed my contractions and when they became regular, about 5 minutes apart, we left for the hospital.

After a routine examination, the nurses got me comfortable in the labor room, and when they told Bob it would be a while, he left and went to have dinner with our friends. All that time I kept looking for him to come and encouraage me! He was afraid he would pass out so he avoided delivery rooms. As the contractions came more often, I could feel the baby's head move down the birth canal, but the young woman who was attending me evidently didn't have experience. When my water broke she came to look, but said, "No, I don't see anything" and went back and sat down. Suddenly an extra strong contraction came, and I felt the baby's head move down considerably. Just then a nurse came in to check me, saw I was completely dilated, and went into action. The large door was opened, I was wheeled into the delivery room, lifted onto the birthing table and into position, and another hard contraction came. A few minutes later our second little girl was born weighing 8 lbs, 7 oz. She was a beautiful baby with dark hair, bright blue eyes and legs that sprang back to her abdomen

CHAPTER 15: THE HUFFMAN KIDS

when they were stretched out. We named her Licia, and all the family was overjoyed with such a lovely child in perfect health.

Learning To Obey

At two weeks she followed motion with her eyes, and when we carried her around, she strained to look at her surroundings. She was very active for her age, and began crawling at five months. She particularly enjoyed playing with paper and anything that crackled, so I would give her sheets of cellophane which she couldn't tear or bite off. One day as she was exploring on hands and knees, she discovered her dad's books in the bookcase and began wrinkling the pages as she played. I told her "NO," gave her some toys, and put her back on her quilt. As soon as I turned my back, she made a beeline for the books. Again I told her no and settled her with other toys. Back she went. After several more tries, I waited until she touched the books, then gently tapped her little hand so she would understand. This went on until, on the eleventh try, out of sheer frustration she turned, looked at the books, said "an-un-ah" and never touched her dad's books again! Persistence paid off, and she understood perfectly what I expected of her!

When she was four months old, I went back to the university to finish my fourth year. Bob had graduated in June with a degree in the three-year program, so since I only needed one year to get my degree, we felt the best thing to do was stay and he could take courses leading to a Bachelor of Bible degree. We had to find someone who could take care of Licia mornings and so asked around and found a student's wife who was interested. She had never had children, and loved little babies especially. I felt the Lord had provided her, and things worked out very well both for Licia, who was perfectly content to go to her "nanny" each morning, and for me as I attended classes and studied.

God's Protective Hands

We were accepted by the mission (BIMI) in November of that year, and in March we began traveling occasionally to present the spiritual needs of France. Even though she was only a year old, Licia was a good traveler, and didn't mind meeting new people, staying in other homes, or being the center of attention. When I received my diploma in June, we began traveling to present our burden for France to different churches around the south. We gave up our apartment to save on expenses. So when we were in Chattanooga, we stayed at the BIMI Mission Center in East Ridge in one of the cabins.

CHAPTER 15: THE HUFFMAN KIDS

The Lord protects His Children in marvelous ways even when they are tiny tots. Bob was away for the afternoon, so I put the girls down for a nap, locked the screen door and went next door to the office a few feet away to help stamp tracts. About 20 minutes went by and I kept watch to see if anyone came or went by the office. Suddenly a middle-aged man, who knew the caretakers, walked in with Licia in his arms. I was so shocked to see him with her that I could hardly answer when he asked whose child she was. He told us he had seen her on the median in the center of the 4-lane highway standing there with cars whizzing by. He stopped his car and plucked Licia out of danger and then came to find out to whom she belonged. I took her and set her on my lap, not believing such a thing could happen, and wondering how she got out on the highway. Evidently she was looking for me! I went over to the cabin next door and found a small hole where she might have crawled through. I unlocked the screen door and went in – Lauri was fast asleep and had no idea that her baby sister had been out looking for adventure. I wondered also how she got out to the middle with all the traffic. We'll never know, but surely we saw the protective hand of the Lord on Licia that day!

When we landed in France, she was not quite 2 years old, and adapted with no problem. Lauri went off to school each morning, and Licia helped me around the house. One day I was clearing the breakfast dishes and told her to drink the rest of her hot chocolate. She answered, "I don't want it because it's dirty in the bottom." When her tummy growled one day after dinner, I teased her saying, "Your tummy's talking; what did it say?" Her answer? "I don't know; it's speaking in French!" I deserved that one. But it amazed me that she understood the situation so well at her age.

Licia had no trouble picking up the language; most young children don't. There was only one time being bilingual troubled her. We had just returned to our home in France after being in the US on furlough for 4 months, speaking mostly English. She was in 1st grade, and came home one day the first week of school very upset, and told us, "The teacher asked a question and I knew the answer, so I raised my hand, but when I tried to answer, I couldn't say it in French!" It seems she burst into tears from sheer frustration!

Being very sensitive spiritually, Licia wanted to follow the Lord and live for Him at an early age. At age 5, she expressed her desire to be saved, so she went to her Dad to talk about it. He showed her in the Bible what Jesus said. Then and there she asked forgiveness and made a profession of faith. Bob baptized her at Temple Heights Baptist Church while we were in Tampa, FL where our families lived.

CHAPTER 15: THE HUFFMAN KIDS

As she grew up, we realized that she excelled in just about everything she did. In sports she was very good in athletics and wanted to participate in competitions. We were disappointed to learn that they were held on Sunday morning. There was no way we could take her to the stadium when we had to be there to open up, be available for counseling, and teach the different classes. All through their youthful years, our children learned to give up certain things in sacrifice to the ministry. It wasn't easy for them, and we were always proud and thankful that they put the Lord first and were not openly rebellious, even though at times they rebelled inside.

In high school, Licia left her mark by being original. Instead of taking Latin, she opted for Greek, and only one other student signed up for it. Both of them especially enjoyed having a private professor. For Mardi Gras, students went to class in costumes just for fun. Licia designed and made an outfit that was half punk and half innocent little girl.

For her 16th birthday, Licia planned a party and invited several of her classmates as well as other friends. She wanted it to be different from a "Boum" so planned fun games and special refreshments. She included a time of testimonies by the Christian youth, but the classmates didn't appreciate this and called her "the sect" the rest of the school year.

A Pact With God

High school in France is much more difficult than in the US. When young folks finish they have the equivalent of 2 years at university level, and are required to have studied two foreign languages, one for five years and the other one for seven years. All through the school year they have to study long and hard, including on weekends. Licia was acquainted with another missionary family's daughter who missed many special meetings on Sunday afternoon plus Youth Group on Saturday so she could study. Licia decided that she would trust the Lord for time to study and not miss any meetings if He would help her and bless her. She did and He did! She never missed a meeting and received her baccalaureate with honors!

CHAPTER 15: THE HUFFMAN KIDS

Our three girls singing for the Lord

After graduating, Licia went to the U.S. for a year of study in order to improve her English and become acquainted with her birth country. It was a difficult year for her because she didn't fit in socially. Many girls talked mostly about boys and make-up, while she wanted to discuss philosophy in the two countries and the difference in culture, etc. She made excellent grades, however, and was named in Who's Who in America 1985. At the end of the school year, she bought her ticket to return to France, packed her trunk and several suitcases, and caught a plane to Brussels, Belgium. We drove up to get her and couldn't believe it when she came through the gate with the caddy piled so high we couldn't even see her! She explained, "The customs officer waved me on through and I didn't have to pay for my extra luggage!" So Licia was home!

Medical Studies

In the fall she began her medical studies at the university in Orsay, which is a suburb of Paris on the southwest side. She retained a room in the dorm so she could live on campus. When checking into the price for train and metro each day, we found that it was less expensive to rent a room than to purchase tickets for the month. Living on campus gave her more time to study and she was allowed one subsidized meal per day in the dining hall.

The first year of medical studies is aimed at preparing the students for the final tests in June, and all but the top few are eliminated depending on the number of doctors the country will need a few years later. In this way, the government loosely controls needs of the future. Licia did very well but still had to do the second year. This time she applied herself like never before, and when the results were posted, Licia was second to the top out of 360 in the class! We were so proud and happy for her! She had really worked hard.

That summer she worked at Calberson's as a trilingual telephone dispatcher, and used her salary to pay for driver's training in order to get her

CHAPTER 15: THE HUFFMAN KIDS

driver's license. Then in September it was back to Orsay to begin serious medical studies.

All during those two years, Pascal was in the picture and their relationship developed into something lasting. They planned a family dinner to announce their engagement and set October 7, 1989 for their wedding—2 years later. (For details on their special day, see the chapter on Weddings)

Bob and I have been conscious of the blessing that each one of our children has become, and many times over have thanked Him for them. They each, in their own way, have been an asset to the ministry God gave us.

Lance

Our only son was born in France, in 1970, a year after our landing. During my pregnancy I had a problem with water retention, and hot flashes, so often opened the window to breathe some fresh air. Since my French still needed to be worked on, I went to a gynecologist at the American Hospital in Neuilly-sur-Seine. My contractions began two days after Lance was due, and he was born early on the morning of March 10. All had gone well for his birth, but the next day he developed a fever of 104°. There was no special room for sick newborns, therefore Lance was transferred to a pediatric hospital in Paris. He weighed just over 4kg at birth, so when they put him in a tiny glass bed for preemies, he filled it completely and could barely move. My doctor let me check out early so I could go see Lance in Paris. Upon arriving home I rented a "tire-lait" in order to keep extracting my milk so I could continue nursing him when he came home. After 10 days we brought him home, but by then he was so used to a baby-bottle that he wouldn't make the extra effort to nurse. He had some digestive problems which took a while to clear up, but with the help of a pediatrician, the problems were resolved.

The girls were enchanted with their baby brother, and he was a calm, happy boy. That summer we drove to the Alps, where Bob had gone the summer before, and stayed in a chalet for a fortnight. It was a relaxing vacation but also allowed us to test our conversational French, since we took our meals in the dining room with the campers. The girls broke out with 3-day measles, so we isolated them a few days, but still took walks on the beautiful mountainside.

Lance developed normally, and was content to play alone while his sisters were away at school. At meal-time he would often go to sleep before finishing completely, so I would put him down for his nap, and often, when he woke up, I would find a morsel of food still in his mouth.

When he was 2 we moved from the apartment to the house on rue du Coq, where he

CHAPTER 15: THE HUFFMAN KIDS

began playing with lego bricks for long stretches of time. While Tom and Linda Butz were with us that summer, Tom got down on the floor many times to build things with Lance. He would call out "MOT" when he wanted a playmate, inverting the letters. Since he was still so small, we thought this was cute! He rarely talked, only saying one or two words at a time. The doctors said it was because he was hearing two languages at once, and that later on he would be able to distinguish them. Even when he began kindergarten at age 3½, he didn't communicate, and didn't start talking until he was 5 years old!

Cries In The Night

When his little sister, Leanne, was born, we moved the two older girls downstairs to the bedroom in the basement, and put the new baby in with Lance. The first night after I brought her home, she began crying during the night at feeding time. Lance woke up and called out, "Momma, get her!" It took him a while to get used to being interrupted at night.

He enjoyed helping me in the kitchen, and I didn't realize the extent of his observations until we had the Pauleys with us from Congo. I had to be away one morning, so asked the grandmother to watch Lance and to empty the dishwasher and put away the clean dishes. Lance stood in the kitchen and told her where each dish went. She was surprised, and so was I!

At the kindergarten he adapted well, but when he started the first grade, began having difficulties learning to read. The school psychologist called me and asked me to come to the school to discuss the problem, and gave me the number of a child psychiatrist at the medical center in town. I made an appointment, and as we walked into her office, her first words were, "Dyslexia doesn't exist." For me, it looked like we couldn't really work together if she had a closed mind attitude from the beginning, so we never returned.

Just before Christmas, Lance came down with a fever, and our pediatrician prescribed some syrup for him. He got better so returned to school. That afternoon the school called saying he was not well – could we come get him? Bob went to his class to get him, and had to carry him because he could not walk. Once home, we called the pediatrician who suggested that was take him to the Hospital Louis Mourier in Colombes, just across the Seine River, because the pediatric section was known for its excellent care. We went to the Emergency Room where they checked him over, and seeing his symptoms did a spinal tap. Yes, it was spinal meningitis.

CHAPTER 15: THE HUFFMAN KIDS

A Very Sick Boy

They hospitalized him, hooked up the monitor, and began a treatment by intravenous. For a few days things seemed critical. Then, on Friday, the doctors told us there were abscesses in the meninges between the skull and the brain and that they might have to go in and operate to relieve the pressure. Needless to say, we were very much affected by this development. When we got home, Bob began calling some pastors and friends both in France and in the US asking them to pray for Lance. One friend (Mickey Johnson) had a ham radio setup, so using that he sent out messages the world over to other Christians who had ham radios asking prayer for Lance.

The next day we got to the hospital with a big question mark on our faces. How was Lance, we wondered. I walked into his room – no Lance! My heart stopped. The nurse came running in and said, "Lance is playing down the hall." We looked, and there he was playing with miniature cars on the floor with other children. No monitor. No intravenous! What had happened? The personnel explained that his fever had broken and the danger was past – he was doing so much better! Bob and I knew it was the Lord's hand that had healed him, and told the doctor when she said she didn't know what had happened, that God had healed him.

What Next?

They kept him a while longer for observation, and he broke out with an allergic reaction to one of his medications, so they kept him even longer. In all, he spent 36 days in the hospital. The day they released him he had a funny cap on his head when we went to bring him home. My first thought was "what has he got now?" The nurse explained that he had caught head lice from playing with other children, and they had proliferated in the warmth of the hospital. The cap was because of a treatment they had administered. At the house I gave him a warm shower and washed all those ugly bugs out of his hair. He was so thin! Only weighing 15kg at age 7½. We asked him what he would like for supper. Pancakes, was his request. Thus began the long effort to put some weight back on him.

The meningitis left Lance with a facial paralysis on the left side, so when he smiled only the right side moved. His left eye did not stay closed when he was asleep, and he limped slightly when he walked. The doctors assured us that in 3-5 months all would be normal again, and slowly we could see the improvement. It took that long for the nerve endings to grow back Before he went back to school we informed his teacher and the director that the paralysis was temporary. They were very kind and understanding, and had a talk with the children of his class so they would comprehend and

CHAPTER 15: THE HUFFMAN KIDS

empathize with Lance. Re-insertion in the class went well but his metabolism was slow and he had difficulty with his school work. For the rest of the year, the school system made a special effort to help him, so he had someone to review with him while the other children had "busy work."

Winter Camp In The Alps

The following month, we had organized a Winter Camp for the youth group, so packed up and drove several vehicles to Albertville, in the Alpes. A colleague and his wife had a 3-floor chalet (the Gordons) and had invited us to stay there for the week. The drive was about 9 hours, and on the way Lance showed me a blister on his arm. At first sight I knew it was the chickenpox. Oh boy, here we go again! We isolated him as soon as we got to the chalet, and sure enough, he began breaking out all over. Linda had her pediatrician come to the house, and besides the ointment for the blisters, he prescribed a series of gamma globulin injections to re-inforce his immune system. So, while Bob was taking care of the youth, I spent time with Lance in between preparing the meals for the whole crowd of 20 some. We divided the youth into teams and they took turns washing the dishes, so that relieved me substantially. In the mornings, there was a Bible study and free time for ping-pong etc. and the afternoon was spent on the slopes either skiing or sledding. It was our first Winter Camp, and because it was so well appreciated, we decided to have Winter Camp every year.

A week after we got home, guess what? Lance's three sisters all broke out with the chickenpox! Lauri was 15, and since she had been vaccinated in the US, her case was mild. Licia, 11, had such a severe case that I had to put ointment on each blister, and counted 73 on her face alone. We took great pains to avoid scratching so there would be no scars. And yes, Leanne broke out, too, the same day as her sisters with a relatively mild case. Our house was like a hospital for a while!

Something Troubling Him

The fact that Lance had started his education in French schools led us to believe it was better to continue in this way. But the years went by and as he grew and developed he had more and more difficulty keeping up. We knew that something was troubling him, and when he started Junior High, I went for a talk with his homeroom professor. She told us tactfully and gently that Lance could not do the work and would not be able to go to high school later on. At home, at church, and with his friends he was completely normal and at ease. Only one sign gave an indication that there was a problem that affected him; he was a chronic bed-wetter! Before going to bed, Bob would get him up, walk

CHAPTER 15: THE HUFFMAN KIDS

him to the bathroom, then back to bed. Even then I often had sheets to wash the next morning.

Not long after his 14th birthday, we learned of a private school in Germany that offered courses for American children whose parents were in the military. They followed a method of re-enforced study called ACE (American Christian Education) through a series of workbooks. Each child was tested individually, and began at his personal level. He could go at his own speed, and was not allowed to advance until he had mastered the material he was studying. At the end of each booklet there was a pre-test, then a final test. Having a practice test gave the child confidence as he took the final test. This method seemed like it might be something Lance could handle. Bob and I prayed, asking the Lord if this would help Lance. In order to know more, we went to Germany to get more information. While there, we learned that they were offering a training course for parents so they could be supervisors in the home, and that Lance could be tested that week. He had never learned to read in English, which was a disadvantage, but since he wanted to try, they allowed him to take the series of tests. At age 14 he began in 3rd grade. We were concerned that this would affect his ego, but went ahead and registered him as an extension student, ordered all the workbooks he would need until the end of the school year (from April to end of June), then went home to start work. That day we took him out of French public school. From then on, he never wet the bed again! We could see the Lord's hand in all these details, and were so relieved to have found a way to help Lance get a suitable education!

A Well-Rounded Education

Thus we began "home schooling"! We set a time to begin, gave Lance a desk where he could work regularly without too many interruptions, and started each day with prayer, asking the Lord to help Lance understand and retain what he was learning. At first I sat with him, helping him to learn to read English. He had to work every weekday in each of the booklets (5-6) for a certain amount of time or do a certain number of pages. He did well right from the beginning and worked steadily and with application on each subject. For his physical education class, Bob took him to the park to jog with him, but he kept having cramps in his side, so they tried other sports. A few years earlier he had taken piano lessons for a year, but wasn't really interested, so when he asked to learn to play the trumpet, we signed him up at the Music School in town. For his break, he would often go across the street to the gas station and either talk a while or help out, so he was not isolated and had several other interests. He seemed completely relaxed and well-adjusted, for which we were thankful.

CHAPTER 15: THE HUFFMAN KIDS

Lance worked steadily and advanced fairly rapidly, so was soon up to the level of others his age. His grades were good, something that was an enormous encouragement to him, and he seemed to enjoy working this way. We bought a good second-hand bike for him, which he would ride out to surrounding towns to see friends from the church, and he participated in meetings of the youth group each weekend.

In six years he completed the workbooks for 10 levels which were needed to graduate from high school, and, since he had good grades, he was the valedictorian of his class, This required him to make a speech at the graduation ceremony in Germany. He wrote everything out, and we would go out to the church where he could stand behind the pulpit, turn on the microphone, and practice speaking. It was a bit scary for him since he didn't know the others in his class, but he applied himself and it all came out well. Now at age 20, he had to decide what to do in the future.

About that time we received news that Bob's mother, who had lymphoma, had decided not to have any more chemotherapy. She needed someone to be with her, and Bob's brother and sister-in-law both worked. It was decided that I would go for 6 weeks and then Bob was to stay 6 weeks. Her condition deteriorated more rapidly than was expected, and she passed away just 3-4 weeks after I arrived. Bob and Lance made arrangements to fly to Tampa, but Leanne was down south at camp, and preferred to remember her as she had been the last time she saw her.

New Life In The US

After the funeral, we all worked on getting her house cleaned out and ready to sell. It took about a month, after which we were scheduled to fly back to France. Lance told us that even though he had a ticket for the return flight, he wanted to stay in the US. So we made arrangements for him to begin further studies at TTU in Chattanooga where Lauri and Pat lived, and flew back without him.

In order to help pay his school bill and dorm fees, he applied for work with the scholarship program there. He worked long hours and into the night, and with a regular load of classes, he was not able to make passing grades that first semester. The counseling committee gave him a 2nd chance if he could pull his grades up, but it was too much for him to handle, so he dropped out and got a job and a small apartment. Lance eventually bought a car and was adjusting to the American way of life, which he enjoyed, when something happened in France that threw his world into a spin. One morning in the fall when Bob slipped outside to open the front gate, a man in uniform asked if

CHAPTER 15: THE HUFFMAN KIDS

Lance Huffman lived there. Bob answered, "No, he is in the US." And the response: "We are looking for him because he never signed up for military service and he is considered a deserter." What a shock! So we called Lance and told him to sit tight until we could find out exactly what he should do.

I had no idea where to go to get the needed information, so I went to the police station and asked their advice. They gave me the number of some military offices, so I began calling and was directed to a colonel who was able to help us. It was a fact that Lance had never signed up for the French military service because he had registered at the American Embassy for military service in the US. At that time we were led to believe that one could hold allegiance to only one country. It seems we were mistaken. What to do? If Lance returned to France he risked being arrested at the airport, so we told him not to come anytime soon. The colonel told me that Lance needed to go to the French Consulate in Atlanta to pick up the forms that he would need, giving him the choice of either renouncing his French citizenship or returning and giving 10 months of service to France. He didn't know what to do, so we told him to wait a while and we would pray, asking the Lord to guide him and show him His perfect will for the future. One night Lance called and said, "I'm going to come back and do my time in the French military so I can have my

HIS HAND IN OUR LIVES

French citizenship." Saying "yes, I'll come back" has taken an enormous weight off my chest!"

It took a while to arrange everything. We had to alert the French military officials to the fact that Lance was coming so he would not be arrested at the airport. Lance had to sell his car and a few pieces of furniture, quit his job, and give up his apartment. Lauri had room in her attic to store the things he wanted to keep, and offered to take him to the airport the day of his flight.

It was October when Lance landed in Paris. We went to pick him up, and he was able to spend a few days with us before reporting for duty. He went through basic training and was sent to Taverny where, among other things, he did guard duty. Since he lived in the area, he was allowed to come home in the evenings part of the time. He finished his 10 months in July, and one of the first things he wished to do was make application for his French citizenship.

A Real French Citizen

We drove out to Sannois to procure the necessary forms and began to put together the list of documents that were required. When we returned, the woman who took care of his file was on vacation. We waited until she returned, and took the application once again. We thought everything was in order, because for Leanne, who had made

CHAPTER 15: THE HUFFMAN KIDS

application just after her 18th birthday, all had gone well, and two weeks later she received her French ID. But for Lance, the woman told him with disdain, "Just because you served 10 months in the French military doesn't make you French!" and refused to validate his application. What to do? Not despairing we drove home and called the colonel who had previously helped us so much. He could not believe a government official had been so adamant in refusing his ID. He asked for her phone number and indicated that he would call her and set her straight on certain things. So Lance got his papers and officially became a French citizen at age 25.

Next on the agenda: find some training for him! We went to the Orientation Center in town, but there was nothing available. We found different tests he could take, but nothing worked out. So he decided to go to work and try to get hands on training. First, he worked several months at the gas station across the street. That was convenient since he lost no time in trains or metro. It was handy also for the owners to have someone so close by who was very serious, punctual, friendly to customers, and honest. While working there, he continued to put in applications for other jobs. Before Christmas he procured a temporary position at the newly-opened Disneyland-Paris as a "figurant" to march in the Christmas parade. This led to another opening, and then another, and eventually to a permanent position at the Hotel New York, first at the reception, since he speaks English, and then in management for conventions and housekeeping. Now, since he has been there several years, he can take care of just about anything at the hotel, and is a valuable employee.

In the summer of 2000 when This Old House was up for sale, Bob and I purchased an apartment with no extra bedrooms. Lance found a studio in Torcy, not far from Disneyland-Paris, and moved in. It was much more practical and time-saving for him, for the train and metro ride each day took about 4 hours. It was his first apartment and he enjoyed fixing it up with a Western theme. He stayed there until February 2014 when he purchased a 3-room apartment farther east, and began redoing the electricity and painting the shutters. It has been particularly satisfying to his dad and myself that Lance is independent, has his driver's license, is punctual, and is a hard worker. I remember one conversation he had with a counselor at the orientation center in Argenteuil. After asking Lance about his qualifications, his experience, and even his health, he told Lance that because of his meningitis and the slight handicap that it left, all he had to do was make application for help from the government and he wouldn't have to work. Lance jumped up and told him "That's over with! I can work and take care of my own needs!"

CHAPTER 15: THE HUFFMAN KIDS

Then he walked out. Yes, and he's a hard worker too. Bob and I have seen the hand of the Lord more than once in Lance's life, not only through his health and miraculous healing, but also at other times. Once his teacher told me that she was leaving the school in her car just when Lance ran across the street without looking and she had to brake hard to avoid hitting him. Another time he was driving on the freeway on his way to come to our house for a visit and lost control of his car, braked, and ended up completely immobile facing on-coming traffic. Praise the Lord, there was not much traffic, so he got the motor started, turned around and got back into the flow of traffic. You can be sure he was greatly affected, and thankful there had not been an accident! The Lord takes care of His children!

Leanne

After the problems Lance had at birth, Bob didn't think we should have any more children; that three was a good number to bring up and educate. However, I was not done mothering! I realized it was no use pestering Bob; his mind was made up! So I left the size of our family in the hands of the Lord, and continued taking birth control. After a certain age, there can be a risk of blood clots, and since my mother had that problem, the gynecologist stopped my treatment and prescribed something else – which was ineffective. A few weeks later I began to have symptoms that made me think I was expecting a fourth child. Lance was 5 now and becoming more independent. I had prayed for a fourth, thinking it would be good for him to have a little brother or sister to play with.

Sure enough, when I made an appointment with the gynecologist – a little one was scheduled to arrive in December 1975. With this pregnancy I had little nausea, but very early had to wear loose clothes. The first day I wore a maternity top everyone noticed, and we had to laugh because the night before on the news one of the ministers in the government had encouraged the young families in France to have more children so there would be enough workers to support the retirees and aging population. So when I went to the open market, several neighbors asked me, "Is this one for Poniatowski?"

In 1975 having an echography was not known as yet, so no one knew the sex of the fetus beforehand. For a name we had chosen Marc William, but couldn't find a girl's name we both liked. The week of Thanksgiving I began having contractions, and when they became regular, Bob drove me to the American Hospital. My mother was there to help out, so she stayed with Lance and the girls. Unfortunately, my contractions stopped at the hospital so they sent me home. What a disappointment to all! But finally on December 4th

CHAPTER 15: THE HUFFMAN KIDS

we became the proud parents of a baby girl weighing 8lbs 9oz. We had finally decided on a girl's name while I was in labor: it would be Lea Anne – or Leanne, and Bob chose Michelle as a middle name.

A Phenomenon

When they brought Leanne to me after her bath and preliminaries, she had her eyes wide open and her arms crossed over her chest as if to say, "Okay, here I am, Mom!" She had a strong will right from the start; she knew what she wanted and let you know about it! The nurses showed me her hair; it was dark and thick with a blonde streak on top! That was unusual enough, but in addition, she had a bottom tooth. Therefore, she was a bit of a phenomenon in the hospital nursery.

Mme. Martin and her daughter had loaned us a lovely antique cradle in dark wood with white curtains for the first weeks, so when the neighbors came calling to see the new addition, I was happy and proud to show them to the bedroom. She didn't stay in the cradle long, however! By the age of 2 months she already weighed over 12lbs (6 kilos). We had an understanding about biting, and she was doing very well nursing. A second tooth had cut through those first days, so having two teeth at such a young age was quite unusual. Since she was gaining weight so rapidly, we decided to put up her crib so she would have more room.

Once she started crawling at 7 months, we had to watch her closely and teach her not to touch certain things, like Momma's plants. However, she was a determined child, and wanted to do what she wanted to do! One day after telling her "no" several times when she tried to play in the dirt of a plant, I slapped her little hand and set her on the rug with her toys. As soon as I left the room she made a bee-line for that same plant, reached up and grabbed one of its leaves and tore it. I saw her from the hallway; a tiny rebel was in the making. She had to be corrected, so off to bed she went, and stayed there crying until she snuffled and stopped. I couldn't believe one so young could retaliate already! It's a good example of the fact that you don't have to teach youngstesr to do wrong – it comes naturally.

A Pool Of Oil

And, of course, there were moments we couldn't get to her fast enough to avoid an accident or a mess, like the Sunday morning when during the church service in the garage chapel she was hungry, so I took her upstairs to feed her. I put her on the floor a minute while preparing her food, and before I could turn around, she had gotten to the cupboard and knocked over a 3-liter bottle of

CHAPTER 15: THE HUFFMAN KIDS

cooking oil. So there she was sitting in the middle of this huge puddle of oil. I couldn't walk through it for fear of slipping and falling, and I didn't want her to crawl through it; what to do? I grabbed the roll of paper towels and started soaking up the oil – enough to make a relatively dry path, then got to her and picked her up before she moved. In the bathroom I had to change her clothes and get the majority of the oil off her skin with paper towels, warm water, and a mild soap, then dry her hair. The kitchen floor was the next project. Fortunately I had enough paper towels to soak up the rest of the oil. You can be sure that when I bought oil the next time, I chose a bottle of only 1 liter, and I put it on the top shelf!

At the age of 10 months Mademoiselle Leanne decided she was done nursing and that she wanted to eat by herself. I tried to feed her with a spoon, but she was extremely independent and wanted the spoon in her hand. Bob and I had always said that we were thankful that our children were relatively clean while learning to feed themselves, but not Leanne! She spread it everywhere, not only on her high chair, but on her clothes, shoes, the floor, in her hair – I never cleaned so much in my life!

After she had weaned herself, she began digestive problems with diarrhea which just got worse in spite of a special diet. I made an appointment with the pediatrician who ordered

HIS HAND IN OUR LIVES

tests. It was found that a staphylococcal germ had settled in her liver, which prevented her from digesting properly. The doctor put her on a fat-free diet plus medication, which included injections. Every time the nurse came several mornings a week, she would cry and hide behind me. It's always difficult to watch one's child suffer, or any child, for that matter! I made a list of foods with little or no fat content, and for 6 months prepared special foods for her. Even on her 1st birthday I baked a sponge cake using 12 fresh egg whites!

After all the special care, she was doing fine, but was still afraid when anyone came to the door, especially a woman. Therefore, when we went to the US for our furlough, she wouldn't let anyone hold her, not even Bob's mother! It took time before she had confidence in anyone except her immediate family.

As she grew and developed, her strong will showed up in areas like choosing her clothes each morning. She definitely had her own ideas, so we learned to compromise. If what she had decided to put on was not suitable for the occasion or the weather, she had to wear what I chose, or we compromised, but it had to be suitable! All this before she turned 3! Certain dresses or outfits were so special to her that even after she had grown out of them, she didn't want to give them away. I had

CHAPTER 15: THE HUFFMAN KIDS

to wait until she was at school before taking anything out of her closet

His Shadow

The year she was two, going on three, Bob and I both went to summer camp to work, so naturally took her with us. Pastor Dedeyan had added a sand pile for the little ones, so she played there mornings while the campers had their Bible studies. At mealtimes, however, she immediately looked for Paul-David, the director's son, and claimed a place beside him. At other times she followed him around, trying to participate in the camp activities. Paul-David was very kind to his little admirer, but I'm sure at times he wished she would just go away!

At age 3 she began kindergarten and adapted well – only going in the mornings, then napping at home. She never had any trouble learning or speaking French because she heard both English and French at home. She enjoyed being with children older than she was, and many times when the youth group had their meetings in our basement meeting room, she would sit at the bottom of the stairs behind the curtain and listen.

When Leanne and Lance – 5 years her senior, played together, Leanne was always the teacher if they played school, and the leader in any other game. She tried to impose her desires in most situations, so we started calling her "la directrice." We had to work with her on learning to let others do what they would like, too.

In primary school she was a serious student, and this continued in Junior High where she studied German as her first foreign language, then Spanish as her second. When we began discussing her high school possibilities, I thought it would be to her advantage to go to a school in a neighboring town where a third foreign language could be added. Leanne refused categorically, saying she wanted to stay in the area where we lived. So she signed up for the High School next to the Junior High, and was able to walk to and from, even coming home for lunch every day. Her grades were very good and when we received her scores for the baccalaureate at the end of her last year, we were proud to see that hers were among the highest that could be attained.

Making Up Her Mind

Now there was only one problem; which branch to choose now? She had signed up for Psychology but realized at the end of the year it was not what she wanted to do. She registered for pre-med in Paris. During that year of studies, she decided that becoming a doctor was not for her, but perhaps another branch in the medical field? As she pondered and we prayed, she thought that for

CHAPTER 15: THE HUFFMAN KIDS

practical reasons she could study to be an English teacher, which would allow her to have the same vacations and work hours as her future off-spring. Besides, she had been teaching English to a group of preschoolers as well as to some teens. This decision was also influenced by the fact that she had had a boyfriend since her last year of high school, and by now they were making plans to announce their engagement. Therefore she registered for English and literature courses and began classes in the fall. By Christmas vacation, however, she was convinced that teaching English was not what she wanted to do.

A Reason To Be Proud!

So during the holidays she ordered courses she could study at home, and in January began studying in her room for 6-8 hours a day preparing to pass the tests to enter mid-wife training. She decided also to take the test for nurse's training so she would be sure and have a place. In April, she went for the test for nurse's training and passed it with no problem. Then in May, she took the exam for mid-wife training. Bob and I were both proud and impressed by her determination in studying alone all these months! And it paid off! Early in July we were at camp when we got a phone call from Leanne saying that not only had she passed the exam, but that she was 19th from the top and therefore would have the choice of the school and hospital to study in. She chose Suresnes, partly because it was one of the best, and partly because it was more easily accessible by commuter train and metro than the others.

Thus began a career of bringing babies into the world, and caring for newborns and their mommies. Her dad would ask her when she came home from a long night of birthing, "Well, how many babies did you have last night?"

Sebastien had come into her life one day when she had baked a batch of chocolate chip cookies and taken them to school. He and his friends sampled them and he thought it would be nice to get to know that American girl who made such tasty cookies. We had always encouraged our children to bring their friends to the house, so, as the end-of-the-year exams loomed on the horizon, several of them came asking for help with reviewing their English. Sebastien came, too, and Leanne invited him to our church services. After several weeks he made a profession of faith and began coming regularly. Bob and I were thankful because God's Word, the Bible, teaches that we should not be unequally yoked with unbelievers, and that includes in marriage. Their relationship bloomed, and a year later they announced their engagement.

CHAPTER 16: THREE WEDDINGS

"Thou wilt shew me the path of life: In thy presence is fulness of joy; at thy right hand there are pleasures for evermore." Psalm 16:11

Only with special help from the Lord were we able to plan, organize, and be successful in having two weddings in one month, one in the US and one in France. It was a race with time, but our Lord took care of every detail.

Licia and Pascal had set their wedding date for October 7. Since we were scheduled for a furlough that summer, in March, Licia and I went to Paris to choose the fabric for her wedding dress. First I made a mock dress out of inexpensive white cotton fabric in order to get the fit just right. Then I cut out and sewed the white peau de soie, adding an original design by Licia of tiny pearls on the bodice (bell skirt, puff sleeves, satin brocade bolero). About this time, Lauri, who was working in a children's home in the US, began telling us about a young man she had met while out walking her dog in the park and who went to her church.

Later on in the spring, the young man called and asked to speak to Bob. Yes, he asked for Lauri's hand, and said they were setting the date for early September. Wow! Another wedding! Of course we were so happy for them, and were more than ready to do all we could to help them. Therefore, I booked my flight a month earlier than the family in order to make Lauri's bridal outfit and two of the bridesmaid's dresses. Problem: where would we stay? Lauri only had one room at the children's home; not exactly large enough for a family of five!

A House For Furlough

We had already asked God to work out all the details, and He worked overtime on this request. One of the ladies in Lauri's Sunday School class learned of the need, and because her husband had recently left her and asked for a divorce, she was living alone in a big house. She offered her home to us for the time needed, and even set up her sewing machine in the office! It was a perfect setup, and we were overwhelmed by her kindness and generosity.

Lauri and I went shopping for fabric, patterns, and notions for her wedding dress. She chose white satin for her dress with full skirt, princess waist, and short puff sleeves. For the maid of honor and bridesmaids, she found a chintz with large light green flowers and leaves on a light background. My priority was to finish the wedding dress before Bob

CHAPTER 16: THREE WEDDINGS

and the family arrived and we began traveling to report to our supporting churches.

It was hanging in the office, all ready and pressed when they landed. Next step: the bridesmaid's dresses. Out of the five, I only had two to cut out and sew, for Licia and Leanne. I asked the Lord to provide a sewing machine in working order wherever we stayed on our travels, and He did! By the end of the summer all the sewing was finished, including a dress for the mother of the bride! And we had traveled several thousand miles in at least 8 states!

Decorations For The Ceremony

Back in Chattanooga it was up to us to plan and provide a dinner for those participating in the ceremony after the rehearsal. In addition, the bride and her "court" were responsible for decorating the church and reception hall. There again, the Lord provided in an unbelievable way. A Christian couple who had visited the church and ministry in France learned about the wedding, and since they owned a business that sold all kinds of artificial flowers, they offered to provide as many as we needed! And they would be going through Chattanooga in their camping trailer, so would deliver them in person! Lauri drew a design of her desired decorations, made a list of the flowers with colors, and sent it off. Our friends brought several boxes of beautiful flowers and the decorations were gorgeous! To top off the blessings, God provided rooms at the conference center where Pat was employed. Therefore, all members of both families, plus friends, stayed in the same place, making transportation simpler and allowing more time for getting to know each other.

At last, the day of the wedding arrived! Licia and Pascal had flown in from France, our family had driven up from Tampa area, Pat's folks were there from Washington State, my dad and new wife from Utah, my aunt and uncle from NC, and friends were there from all over. The bride was radiant and her dress becoming – just the style for her! A friend from their church sang "May all who come behind us find us faithful" which we had not heard before, and it has come to mean a lot to me. Before the bride and groom shared their promises and pronounced their vows, the two sets of parents went forward with candles and lit the unity candle, which was new to us also – so touching! When they began repeating their vows, tears started running down Pat's cheeks. Lauri reached up and carefully wiped them away. By that time he was not the only one shedding tears! Such a moving ceremony!

CHAPTER 16: THREE WEDDINGS

Lauri and Pat

After the wedding there was a luncheon served by the members of Lauri's SS class, a time for photos, and a time of fellowship. Because many had come from afar, Pat and Lauri decided to have a cook out that evening, and spend time with family and friends during the afternoon when they would open their gifts. They left that evening for their honeymoon at a Christian conference center that was not in use for that season in Georgia.

A Second Wedding

Two days later we were on our way back to France! Not only did Leanne have to get back for school, we had another wedding in 4 weeks! Our trip was without incident, but Licia and Pascal got stuck in New York after their plane from Atlanta was late because of bad weather. The ticket office was closed at that time of the night and the company they were flying with had no more flights that night. Thankfully, they were able to purchase tickets with another company, so finally got home after several frustrating moments. The tickets were never reimbursed, so we harbor a bad memory of that company.

After our systems got over jet-lag, we plunged full-time into preparations for Licia and Pascal's wedding. The largest hurdle was deciding on the final menu for the reception buffet and baking the cakes for about 200 guests. That meant hours and days in the kitchen where I baked cake after cake and put them in the freezer. We purchased fruit juices, punch, and the necessary ingredients for tiny sandwiches, jello salads, other fruit for pies, and fresh white tablecloths to drape on the tables. Dear friends from the church prepared accras and other specialties from

CHAPTER 16: THREE WEDDINGS

Martinique and Guadeloupe, and a fellow missionary wife brought over one hundred delicious donuts, so light they melted in our mouths, made from her special recipe. At that time donuts were not available in France. Everything looked so delicious!

In between baking sprees, cleaning and getting the house ready for company was next on the list of priorities. Lauri and Pat were coming, not only for the big day, but to spend their honeymoon, and my dad and his wife Jeanie would be arriving from the States, as well. It was nice to have family around, and we spent many enjoyable moments while working on preparations. Jeanie is very talented manually, and she helped make a good many of the decorations.

Finally the big day dawned. Because our next meal would be hours away, I rose early and prepared pancakes, sausages and eggs for everyone, then began whipping the egg whites for the icing on the wedding cakes. We had several cans of grated coconut that we brought back from the US to embellish part of the cakes at the request of Licia who particularly appreciated it, not only because of the taste, but also for the fluffy look it gave to the cakes.

The weather was cool and humid, a typical autumn day in the Paris area, and the frosting with egg whites and sugar syrup did not whip up and hold its shape like it usually did, so I doubled, then tripled, the quantity needed. Finally, the thick icing rose to the top and the liquid sank to the bottom so I was able to use the thick creamy part by skimming it off. What a relief! Praise the Lord I had enough eggs!

A Forgotten Bouquet!

After everyone had breakfast and had gotten dressed, I went upstairs to help Licia with her bridal outfit. She was beautiful, and I have always been so proud to be her mom. We loaded the vehicles with the drinks and food, etc. and set out to cross Paris to Bondoufle where the civil ceremony at the courthouse was scheduled. Some friends from the church were following us, so there were several cars trying to stay together. Suddenly, Licia cried out, "my bouquet!" She had forgotten to go by the florist's shop to pick it up! We had gone several kilometers already and turning back would have made us late for the ceremony, so we pulled off, after flashing lights all around, and asked a young couple from the church to return for it! They made a U-turn to go back while we continued on, arriving on time, but having to wait for the mayor and company. The civil ceremony, which is required by French law, only took about 20 minutes followed by the signing of the register by the bride and groom and their witnesses. Because it was cool even late morning, Licia was glad to have her satin brocade

CHAPTER 16: THREE WEDDINGS

jacket (bolero) that we had decided to add just in case.

From there we drove to the church in Fresnes, where they had chosen to be married because Pascal's church was not large enough, and neither was ours. Licia and Pascal had designed the programs to be handed out in the entry way, and had even translated the songs into English for those that came from the US. Licia had chosen to have only flower girls and no bridesmaids, and the three little girls looked like models in their light green dresses.

Licia and Pascal

Both the bride and groom were musically inclined; therefore they had written a song which they sang to each other. It was especially touching. Then, after the promises, Bob gave a benediction and they kneeled on satin cushions made by Licia and dedicated their new life together to the Lord.

After photos in a nearby park, the newlyweds joined us at the reception hall. Several of the ladies from their church had prepared finger-foods and a couple had volunteered to set up the table, heat things up, and fill the platters when needed. Pascal's dad, a former baker, had made a gorgeous basket out of cream puffs, and decorated it with Jordan's almonds. It was beautiful, and so good, too.

While the guests arrived, I was busy in the kitchen frosting the cakes and arranging them on a special stand before covering them with the coconut. They looked like round clouds when finished. We spent an enjoyable evening interacting with the guests, sampling the various foods and taking part in the games program prepared by friends of the bride and groom. It was a memorable day! They returned to their studio in Orsay to continue their studies, and put off their honeymoon until later when they would have free time to enjoy it!

CHAPTER 16: THREE WEDDINGS

Leanne And Sebastien, Nine Years Later

After finishing high school, Sébastien worked all summer and then began his studies to be a nurse at the hospital in Argenteuil. He continued working part-time on weekends and a few months before they got married, he bought a 4-room apartment as their future home. We felt this was a very wise move, and to encourage them, we helped out with the renovations and painting. Leanne also worked summers as a cashier in a large store. This made her realize it was definitely not what she wanted to do all her life!

When she was in her 3rd year of mid-wife studies, they set their wedding date for August 29, 1998. I asked her to do one thing: make a special effort to finish her 4th year and receive her diploma. She did, even though it was more difficult with a husband, an apartment to keep up, meals to plan and prepare, etc.

Leanne was undecided about the style for her bridal gown, so while in Lille with Licia one day, we visited a bridal shop where she tried on several styles. She settled on one that, with a few changes, would be satisfactory. The following week we went to Paris to purchase pattern, material and notions for her dress. She chose an off-white peau de soie for a dress with a round neckline, cap sleeves of lace and floor-length skirt mounted on a princess style bodice of lace with hand-sewn pearls in the center of each flower. The skirt had two sheer overskirts, and her veil was gathered at the crown, falling gently over her shoulders on each side of her face. She was a lovely bride!

As they made their plans, they decided to have the civil ceremony at the city hall in Argenteuil on the Friday before their wedding day on Saturday. Leanne found a simple sheath with bolero in light blue, which matched her eyes, and just family and close friends attended. We teased them saying "What day do you celebrate your anniversary, the 28th or the 29th?"

Extra Busy Day

The next day there were so many events to fit in that it had to be the busiest day of their lives! Getting dressed with all the family "camping out" all over the house made it a challenge! Lauri and family from the US were here, plus Lance. Licia and family came in later. Sebastien's brother, Selim, surprised us by arriving with his mother in a limousine. They came in and, as was the custom in Lebanon, gave Leanne a lovely necklace to wear with her bridal gown. Then they whisked Leanne and part of the family off to the church. The religious ceremony was held in an Evangelical Protestant church in a neighboring town because our meeting place behind the house was much too

CHAPTER 16: THREE WEDDINGS

small, and parking was next to impossible. The church had a very nice interior with plenty of room for all who attended to fellowship and enjoy the refreshments.

Leanne had chosen her nephew, Corentin, age 5, to be the ring-bearer, so he had a small cushion with the ring tied on by satin ribbons. At the last minute, he became unsettled and a bit scared about standing up in front of all those people. His dad reassured him and he did all right in spite of his fear. For the flower girls, her nieces Aloïce and Jessica, ages 7 and 6 respectively, wore off-white dresses with blue flowers and blue boleros. The pattern and material were chosen by Leanne and hand-sewn by her sisters.

Third Daughter

Bob gave his third daughter away, walking her down the aisle and then presiding the ceremony. Special music was presented by Pascal who sang one of his compositions, Jean-Claude G'baguidi shared God's Word during a brief message, then, just before they exchanged their rings, Leanne sang a special song to Sebastien as a surprise. The ceremony was crowned with a prayer of benediction by the bride's dad, who mentioned in passing that the bride and groom had decided during their engagement to keep themselves pure until their wedding night. This declaration caused several of their friends and fellow students from the hospital to comment, saying they didn't know how they waited! It was a vibrant testimony to many.

Léanne and Sébastien

A reception was held in the fellowship hall after a picture-taking session, where we all enjoyed the many and varied hors d'oeuvre provided by friends and church members. The families then drove to a lovely park (Bagatelle) where a series of photos were taken.

Several weeks before the wedding, Sebastien's mother had asked them specifically to be married in her church, the Catholic Church. They had already planned things, but to keep peace in the family, decided to add a short ceremony for his

CHAPTER 16: THREE WEDDINGS

mom's sake. So off we went, throwing coins to the bride and groom instead of rice as they exited the edifice. By then we were ready for a rest, but had to get to the hall they had rented for their wedding supper and main reception.

It took much coordination and explanations to make sure everyone arrived at the right place, which was out a distance from town. Since the grounds were attractive, more photos were taken before going inside. Friends of the bride and groom had done a lovely job of decorating, and the yards of netting I had found at the open market looked like clouds overhead. The tables were draped in white linen and graced with baskets of white flowers set off by the greenery. White lattice work sported cascading branches of ivy and several baskets of flowers brought by guests were placed in front of the bride and groom's table.

Besides a lovely catered dinner, there were cute games for the newlyweds, peaceful background music by Lance, the bride's brother, and later in the evening, a waltz for the bride and groom. Our family left soon after midnight, but many young people stayed on until the wee hours.

Three girls, three bridal gowns to sew and three beautiful weddings: who could ask for more blessings? We are thankful that each daughter married a Christian and that they are bringing their children up to know and love the Lord and to be faithful to their church. God has abundantly blessed our family!

Since their weddings, our daughters have presented us with eleven grandchildren: nine by natural birth and two by adoption. We praise and thank the Lord for each one!

CHAPTER 17: BOB'S YOUTHFUL YEARS

"We will rejoice in thy salvation" Psalm 20:5

Born into the Huffman family on June 14, 1938 in Findlay, Ohio, Robert Eugene was the second child of Helen and Clarence Huffman. His brother Bill was 18 months older, so they did many things together. The boys were 5-6 years old when their dad left for another woman. Helen went to work as a waitress in a restaurant and since she was gone most evenings until late, the boys stayed often with their maternal grandparents.

Helen remarried a few years later, so the boys grew up knowing their step-father, Tang, better than their dad. He, too, worked nights, so at times the boys went to bed early, but not to sleep, and as soon as the coast was clear they would get up, get dressed and go out. One evening Bill went with a buddy and Bobby begged to join them. He would tell on Billy if he couldn't go with them. The three of them filled their pockets with pebbles and climbed a large tree that had a big branch growing out over the street. Quietly they waited until a car came by then dropped pebbles on the windshield. Fortunately, there were no cracked windshields but they got scared when one man got out of his car to look around, and never tried that again!

Heard The Gospel

On Saturdays they began attending a Bible Club taught by an older pastor in a nearby church, and heard the Gospel for the first time. Some of the children were not very well behaved, and Bob remembers what a hard time the pastor had in keeping the group calm enough for the lesson. But he heard of Christ's love and sacrifice for him, which brought forth fruit in later years.

When the boys got older the family purchased a farm just out of town, and, in addition to a vegetable garden, fruit trees and strawberry beds, they had a couple cows in the barn across the road. The boys had to carry water across the road for the livestock because there was no water in the barn or on that side of the road. The water pipes only ran to the house. The school bst drove by to pick them up each morning, and one of their delights was to "spill" a bucket of water on the steep side of the road, in winter, watch it freeze, and then watch the bus try to get up there to pick them up. One spring the boys each got a calf and raised it to take to the fair for showing.

One year, when Bob was about 8 years old, his uncle Charles asked him to show his raccoon in the wild animal division. The raccoon was on a leash, so all Bob had to do was walk him around the stand in front of the judges. The poor animal got

CHAPTER 17: BOB'S YOUTHFUL YEARS

frightened and tried to get away by climbing up Bob's leg. Bob wasn't too well acquainted with wild raccoons, so he shook his leg to get him off. The raccoon kept climbing back up, and Bob continued to shake him off. I don't know if they won a prize, but the audience was in stitches. Even the judges were laughing!

Defending His Territory

Billy and Bobby slept in a double bed, and to make him scream, Billy would throw his long legs over on Bob. Little brother got smart and sharpened his toenails to a point. When Bill's legs came over on his side, Bob jabbed him with his "daggers," warning big brother to stay on his side of the bed!

Mother was afraid the work on the farm was getting to be too much for the boys, so put it up for sale without telling them, and they were really mad and upset about leaving the farm. They bought a house trailor and then moved to Florida. The grandparents had retired by then and were living in the Tampa area. They finished their junior high years and went on to high school at Brewster Technical High, where Bill was a student in the machine shop, and Bob learned to run presses and set type in a print shop. By that time Bill and Bob had developed different interests, so, after graduating, Bill went into the Air Force as an airplane mechanic, and eventually was sent to

Okinawa. A year later, after Bob received his diploma, he, too joined the Air Force and upon completing basic training in Texas, was sent to Miami as a chauffeur for the bigwigs. He was later sent to Tripoli, Libya where he was stationed at a base way out in the desert called Ben Ghazi. It was there that he began attending church services regularly at the Chapel, and gave his heart and life to serve the Lord after being baptized in the Mediterranean Sea.

It was the beginning of Bob's personal relationship with the Lord and of his calling to serve Him. Because of the time he had served in the Air Force overseas, he was given an "early out," so returned to Tampa and began looking for a job, and a girl to date. (The rest of his life story is found beginning in Chapter 1 of this book.

CHAPTER 18: GAIL: GROWING UP

"Remember not the sins of my youth... Remember thou me for thy goodness sake, O LORD." Psalm 25:7,8

Nothing in my childhood indicated that my life would be dedicated to serving God. My parents met at a horticultural school and married after finishing. The first of three, I was born a year later just after they had purchased a dairy farm in Piermont, NH. I can remember riding the cows home from pasture and into the barn across the road from the house. My brother Richard was born almost 3 years later, then my sister Carol the following year. The farm was too much work alone, so my dad sold out and we moved into a cottage just down the road.

I started school in a 2-room schoolhouse: grades 1-6 met downstairs, grades 7-12 upstairs. The next summer we moved to East Longmeadow, MA where I was in 2nd grade, and it was there that we attended a Baptist church one Sunday, and at 7 or 8 years old I heard the Gospel for the first time in Sunday school. The story of Christ's redemptive life, death, and resurrection was illustrated using

HIS HAND IN OUR LIVES

flannel graph, and it had a definite influence on my thinking.

Childhood Maladies

Because my brother had heart problems after being ill, the doctors encouraged my parents to move to a milder climate. My Dad's parents had previously moved to Florida to retire, so this was a natural choice. I remember that the movers came and packed our furniture and belongings in a huge truck, and we were supposed to leave a few days later after spending time with Momma's parents, when I came down with the measles. The doctor said no traveling for 2 weeks, so we stayed on until I got better. Or course upon arriving in Florida both my brother and sister came down with the measles, and they had to stay in a dark room instead of playing in the warm Florida sunshine.

500 Cheepers

My parents purchased a small frame house on 5 acres in Dover, and we moved in after staying those first weeks at the Branch Ranch, Plant City. We got registered for school and had to ride a school bus ten miles to the grammar school in Plant City. My dad got a job in construction working on the Jai-Alai Fronton in Tampa. His folks eventually brought their house trailer from Orlando and parked it on our land. My dad decided to use the acreage for a chicken farm, so built 2 huge coops and

CHAPTER 18: GAIL: GROWING UP

bought an incubator. A truck delivered 500 chicks, which we had to feed and water before and after school. This was a novelty to us, and we enjoyed the "fluff balls" that peeped constantly. They grew too fast, however, and at nine weeks the young roosters already had their cock's combs and were learning to crow. At first it sounded like they had a sore throat!

One night a truck came after dark, after the chickens had settled on their roosts, and took all the little roosters to be prepared for the meat counter at the grocery. The pullets were left to become laying hens. Dad built nesting boxes along the center wall of the coop out of strong orange crates, and padded them with straw where they could lay eggs.

Another 500 chicks arrived, and we started the process again. When the young hens began laying, we gathered the eggs in a large rubber-coated basket and washed each egg individually with vinegar water, weighed it (small, medium, large or extra-large), and then put them in large boxes according to their size. On Saturday mornings a truck came with the chicken feed for a week, and took the eggs to market. As the flock grew, so did the amount of work. Since both of our parents worked, Gramps and Grandma Blanchard were overseers when we helped after school, but I'm sure they did more than their share during the day. Not only were there eggs to gather, wash and weigh, there were water jugs to clean and fill, and to feed the hens we took big buckets of cracked corn, called "Here, chick, chick, chick," and then scattered the corn far and wide so all the hens had access to some feed. This was done because of pecking order as some hens lorded it over others and chased them away. We had to rescue some poor tortured hens and isolate them so they would survive.

Plentiful Crops

Our chickens were white leghorns that laid white eggs. Some of them became very tame and squatted down with their wings spread out slightly waiting to be patted. I don't know if this was unusual or not. My mother was a great animal lover, and tamed every animal we had. For those few years on the farm, we also had a milk cow, a couple of pigs that were slaughtered, a calf that was bucket-fed to be put in the freezer, and of course, a dog. The vegetable garden yielded beans, peas, corn, beets, lettuce, tomatoes and we had guava bushes. Down the road was an orange and grapefruit grove, a cabbage farm and a strawberry farm. Every spring we spent our Saturdays picking strawberries, putting lots in the freezer. And in the fields around us there were huckleberry bushes (similar to blueberries). As we walked through them

CHAPTER 18: GAIL: GROWING UP

we could pick and eat, but sometimes we took a container and picked enough for a pie or muffins.

The Simple Life

Life was simple and healthy, and the three of us grew tall and strong. We walked a mile morning and afternoon to catch the school bus; crossed the pasture to the neighbors' and swam in the creek all summer, went to the beach some weekends, and played outside almost every day. Dad built a tree house for us, and with the extra railroad ties that he had used for the frame of the chicken coops, he put up a temporary log cabin for us to play in. Of course, we helped with other jobs, in addition to cleaning eggs and feeding chickens. When Dad built on to the house, doubling the size of it, he put down a parquet 8 inches x 8 inches square in alternate squares, and our job was to sand it down before he varnished it. As the oldest, I had more responsibility, so I was asked to mow the grass on part of the 5 acres, to cook some meals when Momma was working, to hang up laundry and to iron it, and to clean house and wash dishes.

Before the addition was built on, we lived in a square frame house divided into 4 rooms, with an outhouse down the path outside. We took our bath outside in late afternoon in a galvanized tub, and a teakettle of boiling water warmed up the well water. When Dad got the inside bathroom installed, we could really appreciate it!

Not long after he finished the addition to the house, he sold the farm and we moved to Temple Terrace near Tampa. This was the end of our childhood in a happy environment. Dad built a small house for Gramps and Grandma on the other end of the property – a plot he had saved for them, - and we began to get used to life in town. This situation didn't last long, for the following spring Momma took us to court with her and divorced Dad. She was awarded custody of the three of us, but a few weeks later we woke up and she was gone, bag and baggage. Dad contacted the judge, who gave him custody of us and he got the house back. I don't remember how Richard and Carol reacted, but I pretty much kept it all inside, not knowing how to exteriorize my feelings.

A Fractured Family

Living with Dad only gave us, especially me, more responsibility than ever. Richard and Carol (ages 9 and 8 respectively) each had their jobs, but I had to take over running a household at age 12. I learned fast, though, and soon was preparing well-balanced meals regularly, doing the grocery shopping, and taking care of laundry, ironing and cleaning. Since Dad was an insurance salesman at the time (he was a jack of all trades and could do

CHAPTER 18: GAIL: GROWING UP

just about anything) he was rarely home in the evenings, but usually came by the house around 5 PM to check on us, give instructions if needed, and bring us a bunch of bananas or box of cookies. For being a single dad, he really made an effort, and we knew he cared about us.

In his business he sometimes had people that couldn't pay him, so he often accepted things or services in place of money. One year he signed me up for ballet lessons, which surprised me since I was not at all graceful. I found out later that the teacher owed him for her insurance. A couple of times he took us on vacation, once for a week at a house on Keystone Lake near Odessa, FL. The owners hadn't been able to pay Dad, so we benefitted from their cabin, their boat and equipment, and had a wonderful time. We thought Dad he would spend the week with us but he kept on working.

One of the neighbors whom Dad knew had a motor boat, and their son offered to teach us to water-ski. When my turn came, he gave me basic instructions, then added, "There are alligators in this lake, so don't let go or fall down." You can be sure I held on tight and didn't fall!

It was while we were at the lake that week that we met the Mallory family whose main residence was on the lake. Carolyn was my age and we went to the same high school. We became friends, and it was Carolyn who introduced Bob to me 3 years later. She invited me to her church the following weekend, and I enjoyed the meeting, the music and the fellowship immensely, regretting that we had to leave soon and that I couldn't continue to attend youth meetings.

A New Church

Back in Temple Terrace we began attending the Community Church, and while there I heard the Gospel again, joined the choir and the youth group, and helped with SS. The pastor taught and preached from the Bible, but when he retired the new pastor had a more "open" mind and talked more on subjects that were attractive to "intellectuals." All this seemed so artificial to me, and I began to lose interest.

For two-three summers, my Aunt Eleanor invited me to spend a couple of months with them in NC. My cousin Lennie was just 9 months younger than I, and we got along famously! Aunt El and Uncle Charles became my second parents, and helped me enormously to get through those difficult teen years. Lennie and I spent hours in their pool, paddling around or racing in inner tubes, splashing and swimming. In the evenings we lit candles set in cork holders, and let them float on the water while we enjoyed company on the deck and the beauty of the flames reflecting on the water. We made

CHAPTER 18: GAIL: GROWING UP

gallons of lemonade and took them to the golf course owned by my uncle where we set up a stand and sold the refreshing beverage to hot and thirsty golfers. With the proceeds, I bought a couple of patterns and lovely end pieces of material and spent hours in my aunt's sewing closet making my wardrobe for the upcoming school year in high school. I had learned to sew out of necessity, for, after Momma left, I began growing and developing so fast that I had almost nothing that fit for that fall when I turned 13. At home I found a piece of flowered cotton material in a closet, bought a pattern and made my first dress at age 12. Momma bought me two dresses, each with a bolero, so I wore each one day with the bolero, and then, one day without, for 4 days, and with the dress I had made, I was able to get thru a week at school wearing something different every day. This was a necessity in FL because the heat made us perspire abundantly.

Learning To Ride A Bicycle

One summer we flew from NC to my grandparents' house in MA with Aunt Eleanor, and while there, Lennie and I found several pieces of discarded furniture in a room behind the garage and made a playhouse after sweeping out the dust. We played for hours in there! We also discovered an old bicycle that had belonged to my mother. Since I had never had a bike, I didn't know how to ride one, so the next logical step was to learn how. In just a few days I was getting around like an old hand, and was disappointed to have to leave the bike when we flew back to NC. What a memorable vacation!

That first summer the hurricane season came early, so Lennie, her brother Jay, and I played board games for days. One of my fondest memories of my time spent there was in the evenings when everyone else was in bed, Jay would go to the piano and play, among other favorites, Rhapsody in Blue by Gershwin. The music not only thrilled me, but it helped us to relax.

But all good things must end, and school would be starting, so it was back to FL. A few days after getting home, a delivery man came with – surprise – my mother's old bike! My grandmother had shipped it down for me! That was so kind of her, and I appreciated it so much!

Out Of Trouble

The following summer Dad decided that, to keep us out of trouble, he would keep us busy! He bought buckets of paint, got out the ladders and paint brushes, and instructed us to brush down and paint the whole outside of our three-bedroom block house. This definitely kept us busy! We worked mostly in the morning before the temperature became unbearable and aimed at finishing a certain

CHAPTER 18: GAIL: GROWING UP

area each day. When we were finished, Richard and I were especially proud of our accomplishment. Carol had helped by taking care of other tasks in the house.

Richard, Carol and I learned much later that Momma had left – not alone – but with a truck driver she had met, and would go with him on his trips. What was sad was that he had a wife and 4-5 children, who suffered from this situation, especially when Momma went to their church. Then we found out she was expecting a baby – which shocked us all. My Dad forbade her to come to the house, so we didn't see her for a long time. She had a girl and named her Sarah Ellen. The Lord chastises, and a couple of years later H. died of cancer, leaving two families without a father. Momma couldn't handle it and had to be put in psychiatric care for a while. Little Sarah Ellen was put up for adoption and we never heard about her again. At the same time, Dad was dating different women so was often gone all evening. Unfortunately, one was a married woman. Her husband found out and would come around our house at night looking for her. Several times I found evidence that someone had been there, such as cigarette butts, (no one smoked in our family) and I often heard noise late at night. I can look back and realize how the Lord protected us!

Both Grandmothers

The year I was 15, and in 10th grade, both my grandmothers passed away. Grandma Blanchard had heart trouble, and the day she died in September they called me out of class to tell me. She had always called me Bridget, and taught me to cook and sew. For my Jr. High prom, she had made a blue evening gown with white lace on the bodice, even though it was difficult to sew. At the same time we learned that Grandmother Dibble had had a stroke and was paralyzed on one side. Grandfather Dibble was a Christian Scientist who didn't believe in procuring medical care, so he put her in a home where she only had basic care. She passed away in January without regaining use of her limbs. Both of them were 69. Losing both of them affected me deeply, for both of them had meant so much to me! I had spent a year with Gr Dibble at age 5-6 when Richard was ill with rheumatic fever as a toddler, and she had a definite influence on my spiritual leanings by reading the Bible to me and by sharing its truths. She had also given me my first Bible when I was 12, which I cherished throughout the years. I'm certain she prayed for me especially when our family broke up and the three of us were left alone.

On lonely days, I would go sit on the bank of the Hillsborough River which ran through our town, and talk to the Lord. My awareness of God was not

CHAPTER 18: GAIL: GROWING UP

highly developed, but I sought to know Him better, and had done so since childhood. It is interesting to note that the campus of Florida Christian College was right on those peaceful banks, and much later I learned that Billy Graham had studied and walked there.

Another earth-shaking event took place that fall: our Dad remarried! He had been dating different women all along, but decided to settle down again. Eloise was divorced and had three children – all younger than we were – so that made a full house with 6 offspring! It was great to have someone to talk with that understood, and Richard and Carol benefitted also from having a feminine presence in the home. I had less responsibility therefore and could spend more time on my studies.

I especially enjoyed my classes in Home Economics, and when I completed the project of redecorating my sister's and my bedroom, the Home Economics' teacher came to the house to see it. First of all, I had covered the faded dark green walls with a pale pink paint. Eloise had given us her sheers that criss-crossed at the window, and I had made drapes and bedspreads to match of material with a white background and large pink roses. It made an enormous difference, it really looked like a girl's room.

Because we were all crowded in just 3 bedrooms, Dad and Eloise decided to add on to the house, enlarging the living-dining room and adding a master bedroom with a bath. It was a big project that took several months, but gave enough space for a growing family. About the same time, Dad had the carport built in so Gramps, who was living alone, could live with us. He was good company to Ralphie, who was born to Dad and Eloise in May, my senior year in High school.

Rebellion

Awareness of God, however, was not sufficient, nor did it make a difference in my life or conduct. It took an act of rebellion to awaken me to the fact that even though I had strived to have acceptable conduct and do good, deep down my heart was tainted with unhealthy reactions. For more than 3 years I had directed the household, receiving praise for doing so well at a young age. After Dad remarried, he began scolding me for every little thing I said or did that displeased him or Eloise. Resentment began to build up inside, and I began to think of ways to escape the criticism.

One evening in December I offered to babysit the younger children so Dad and Eloise could go out. After they left, I packed a small suitcase, took the keys to Eloise's car, and drove away, heading north. In town I picked up my boyfriend. Together

CHAPTER 18: GAIL: GROWING UP

we had decided to get married and solve the probems ourselves, and had friends who told us that in Mississippi it was legal to marry at age 16. Both of us were ignorant and just looking for an easy way out of our troubles.

We were mis-informed; no one would marry us. So we headed back south and drove to his uncle's place. He called the police, and we were gently escorted to the police car, which drove us to our respective homes. Dad had reported the car as being stolen, and the police were looking for us all over Florida.

Back Home

Upon arriving at the house, I began to realize all the pain and worry I had caused my family. Of course, the whole neighborhood knew about my disastrous actions, and some had even called to ask questions.

Dad had questions, too, and became so angry that he said, "I ought to take you out back and horsewhip you. You're going to be just like your mother!" The tears started flowing and I went to my room to get ready for bed. Sobbing on my pillow, I began talking to the Lord; "Oh God, I don't want to turn out like my mother! I'm so sorry for all the hurt I've caused! I want to give you my life and follow you!" I felt a sensation of complete peace come over me, and I knew God had heard me and forgiven me. Now I could sleep knowing that God loved me and had a future for me.

The next morning, first of all, I needed to ask forgiveness from Eloise. The night before I had learned that people thought I ran away because I couldn't get along with my stepmother. It seemed so out of character since I loved her dearly, and never wanted to hurt her on purpose. We had a good talk, and I resolved in my heart to help her as much as possible and make things as easy as possible. Also, I wanted to squelch the rumor about stepmothers!

Facing The Music

One of the hardest things I had to do was go back to high school. So many kids looked at me with a questioning look; others looked, then turned away. Because of my "crime," my grades, which were quite good, were docked one level each. In addition, the police set a date for me to appear in juvenile court before a judge. That was scary!

The rest of my junior year was uneventful, as such. My desire was to pull my grades back up, and do everything possible to alleviate the shame I felt for the hurt I caused my family. As the days passed, I realized one important aspect of my "adventure." Before, I thought I was surely good enough to earn my place in heaven, for I had never done anything to disobey or bring shame to my

CHAPTER 18: GAIL: GROWING UP

parents. Now, I knew I was a bad girl deep down, with no thought for others: an egotistical "sinner" was what I was. I began to read my Bible, and soon learned of the sacrificial death on the cross of Jesus, the son of God. My brothers and sisters still attended the Community church in Temple Terrace, so I returned, hoping to learn more about God and the Bible.

Although I was quite ignorant of the Christian way of life, when things did not seem right, there were flashing red lights in my brain. My parents asked me to go have a talk with the pastor. I complied, and listened. When he said that life was just a series of circumstances without necessarily any plan from above, it sounded so out of character of the God I was just getting to know! I left, disappointed that a pastor could have so little faith in the Lord.

At the end of the school year, I found a part-time job keeping three little children for a couple who both worked afternoons. The money I earned was enough to purchase contact lenses and my school clothes. When I started my senior year, no one knew who I was because they had never seen me without glasses. It was fun going down the hall saying hello to all my friends, to see their faces! They couldn't place me, not even by my voice!

The highlight of the fall semester was being inducted into the National Honor Society. I had worked hard to bring my grades back up, but was still surprised when they called my name! My parents had been notified and were in the back of the auditorium, proud and happy that I had turned out all right after all! Yes, it had been a difficult period for our combined families to get through, but looking back, I could see the hand of the Lord and how He had directed all things! And even though I suffered because of the wrong I had done, if I had not run away, I might never have realized how desparately I needed to be saved! Thank you, Lord, for setting me on the right path!

CHAPTER 19: WHY WE STAYED

"Take heed to the ministry which thou hast received in the Lord, that thou fulfil it."
Colossians 4:17

During the 40 years we served as church-planters in Argenteuil (which is a suburb of Paris), other missionary families came and left after only a short time. Different reasons were brought forth and some families could not understand why we stayed on.

There were several strikes against us from the beginning. We were the only family in France with our mission board, therefore we had no one to help us get started; we were not as cultured as most of the French; and Bob had a difficulty in learning French. He had to apply himself rigorously in order to read, write, and speak well enough to preach messsages.

On the other hand, we had several good reasons to learn French in order to share the Gospel of love and grace with new-found friends and acquaintances. First of all, without a shadow of a doubt, we knew the Lord had called us to France. This knowledge was a great source of security for us! If discouragment came, we could always remember the time we received His call. At the same time, we were not discouraged by what God was doing or what He had done; we could only be discouraged by our own weakness and our lack of zeal and boldness, even by missing an opportunity to witness to someone!

Only One Time

In all the years that we served in France, both of us were so content to serve the Lord that there was only one time we thought maybe the Lord wanted us to leave the ministry. Two or three years after I had a hysterectomy, I began having severe pain in the lower right abdomen. Our doctor checked me over, ordered tests, and prescribed anti-spasmodic medicine even though he found nothing abnormal. The pain became more and more severe, and I needed more and more medication. These spells went on for almost three years, and even several specialists were scratching their heads. My physical well-being was affected, and even if I stayed in bed, the pain did not subside. The doctor prescribed more tests, to no avail; no one had the answer!

Bob brought up the subject of leaving the ministry because I never knew when I would be well enough to teach at Awana Club, Sunday School, or even plan a Ladies meeting! Our doctor sent me to see a gastroenterologist, who, after briefly looking over my records and not even

CHAPTER 19: WHY WE STAYED

examining me, alluded that it was psychosomatic: all in my head! I was so upset! I couldn't believe that he would come to such a conclusion without trying to find a physical reason, or even asking any questions about my family, my work, or my ambitions.

Emergency Surgery

Less than a week later, I woke up on Sunday morning throwing up. I could feel that in my lower abdomen there was no activity. Bob called the doctor on duty and asked him to come by immediately. After examining me and asking some questions, he informed us that he suspected an intestinal occlusion, and told Bob to take me to the emergency room at the hospital.

Since there was already a crowd in the waiting room, they put me on a stretcher out in the hallway and brought a basin because the throwing up continued even when lying down. Physically I was miserable, but inside I was so happy and relieved at the thought that now they would find out the reason for all the pain and spasms. Soon I was taken in for X-rays which showed there was blockage, but they could not determine just what it was. Emergency surgery was ordered and I was taken upstairs to the block.

It may seem unusual to say it, but I was glad they were going to operate. I couldn't help but

HIS HAND IN OUR LIVES

praise the Lord for it seemed the end of the suffering was at hand. I sang praises to the Lord silently, and repeated over and over, "Thou will keep him in perfect peace whose mind is stayed on thee." Isaiah 26:3 I'm sure the medical staff never saw a happier patient!

The next morning when the surgeon came by my room, he explained what the problem had been. Previous surgery had caused the peritoneum to tear, letting part of the colon slip out through the opening and get twisted around. This had gone on for more than three years, causing the colon to become so accustomed to this that it began having spasms even when it was not compressed. This particular ailment is called the Speigel hernia and is relatively rare, which is why the doctors and specialists were unable to diagnose the problem.

I had been put in a private room, and learned that one of my nurses was the wife of my son-in-laws' best friend. She was so kind and gentle and well-appreciated by both patients and staff. My son-in-law, Sebastien worked in the emergency room and told his co-workers that I was there, so one by one they all came by to say hello and wish me a speedy recovery. The church members came by as did many of my neighbors, so there was no time to get lonely! After 10 days I was finally able to eat and drink without losing it, so was allowed to go home.

CHAPTER 19: WHY WE STAYED

The following Sunday I shared a testimony in church of how God had taken care of me by allowing the occlusion so the real problem could be found. My health so improved that I was able to resume my part of the children's work, ladies meetings and visitation. Neither Bob nor I ever mentioned leaving our ministry again.

Ten Years

There were other reasons as to why we stayed. One, the Lord never told us to leave. We tried as best we knew how to follow His will, and and we see why in retrospect. Staying in one town and continuing to witness to the same people was the best thng we could do. In France it takes a very long time to become real friends with someone, and they are suspicious if you become too familiar too soon. So God planted us in Argenteuil where we took the time needed to build solid relationships.

I remember that one lady who lived on our street would not acknoledge me when I said "Bonjour." I continued greeting her even though she wouldn't answer and just walked on past without even looking at me. One day she stopped when our paths crossed and began talking. Before we finished our conversation, I knew her life history! She was so hungry for human contact, but would not open up and allow others into her private world. It had been ten years since I first spoke to her!

Each time we moved we made a point to stay in touch with our former neighbors. In addition, we send out New Year's card to all of them, and tried, by an occasional phone call, to stay abreast of their family news. Because of this we have been able to call them and invite them for special meetings or concerts, and many have attended. And, of course, I take advantage of sending cards to include a tract or short message. They definitely know that we believe the Bible and try to live by it's principles.

There are other reasons as to why we stayed, like the children's education. It was very difficult for them to miss 3-4 months of the school year in France when we took a short furlough, even though they took courses by correspondance. So in order to have a continuity in their studies, we would go to the US during the summer only.

As mentioned previously in Chapter 14, one of Bob's characteristics was staying with something until it was completed! He could not have envisioned leaving a church-plant until it was mature enough to have a national pastor, and the finances to take care of him and the needs of the church. That is another reason we stayed so many years in the same town; to finish the job!

CHAPTER 19: WHY WE STAYED

However, in thinking about it, the most important reason must be just one four-letter word: LOVE. First all, Love for our dear Lord who gave Himself so sacrificially: how can we do less? The least we can do is give our lives to serve Him, and in doing so, He gives us so much in return!

I sometimes think that if we had just continued doing what we had planned with our lives when we got married, Bob would probably still be working in a print shop, and I would be a teacher, frustrated because nowadays it is so difficult to keep peace in the classroom. Instead, He allowed on-the-job training, travel, gave us friends around the world, and most of all, many French brothers and sisters in Christ. "We love Him, because He first loved us!" I John 4:19. "Beloved, if God so loved us, we ought also to love one another." I John 4:11

What more can I say?

CHAPTER 20: HIS HAND STILL GUIDES

"O LORD, thou art my God; I will exalt thee, I will praise thy name; for thou hast done wonderful things; thy counsels of old are faithfulness and truth." Isaiah 25:1

After my husband passed away, I needed the Lord's help more than ever before. Several tasks that he had always taken care of became my responsibility. One of these was keeping the car running. I had to remember things like gettng it checked every two years as required by the government. (Control technique). Usually the employees are indifferent to car owners, just running the vehicle through the necessary tests. But this time, seeing I was alone, they were especially kind, and I didn't feel threatened because I didn't know every detail.

If I had a problem with an appliance or other, my son-in-law Sebastien would drop by after work, and usually get it straightened out. If not, then he would tell me who to call.

All Those Books!

One of the most difficult decisions I had to make was what to do with all of Bob's books and Bibles. They were so precious to him and I wanted them to go to someone who would treasure them and use them as he had. Many of the old books were those he had found in used bookstores in England when we were there for a conference. The majority were studies of one or more books of the Bible, and were in English.

The only person in our immediate family who preached often was our son-in-law Pascal. My desire was to keep many of the books in the family, so asked him and all the grandchildren if they would like to pick out some to keep and use. To my delight, Pascal was exceedingly happy to increase his library with several practical volumes such as Josephus, and two or three sets with four to five volumes. Our granddaughter found some she wanted to keep, so little by little there began to be spaces on the wall of shelves.

Only a couple of the men in church spoke English, but neither of them did much preaching. There were some books in French which the men at church were pleased to have, so that helped a little. I called the Bible Institutes and offered them books, but they already had too many in English. What to do? I had asked the Lord to help me find those that needed the books, but so far no one had shown an interest. I added this request to my urgent prayer list and asked a few friends to pray with me.

About that time I received an invitation and the dates of the "Mission Possible" Conference held in Germany every fall. In addition to the stirring

CHAPTER 20: HIS HAND STILL GUIDES

messages and the fellowship and encouragement, there was the "clothes closet" with many nice articles of clothing donated by storeowners and fabricants. Since most families appreciated the clothing, why not books?

I asked Mickey and Cookie Johnson if it would be all right to add the books to the "give-aways." They were excited about the possibility of helpng the young missionaries and pastors in this way. So I called Pastor Woody of Rheinland Baptist Church in Landstuhl, Germany. He offered to line up one or two of the military men in his church to come over and pick up the cartons.

A couple weeks later he called and asked if he and one of his men could come over the next day. I thanked the Lord for providing the transportation. It had taken me several days to sort and pack up the many volumes. In all there were 18 large cartons.

After the message on the first evening of the conference, the ladies wandered over to look through the garments, and the men to peruse the study books. Several of the men came over to show me what they had found and to share the fact that they had wanted to procure some books for a long time. One young missionary with tears in his eyes told me what an enormous help this was because his office was above the garage which had caught fire and all his volumes had burned. He was very appreciative of the possibility of replacing some and acquiring others.

The Lord guided me also in using the finances wisely and for His glory. Bob had left a sum of euros in the work fund and told me to use this money in a way that would help the church and the ministry. I put this decision before the Lord, and a few months later felt He would have me use it to help in training our young Christians for service to God. I found out that several desired to take the training required by the govrnment in order to work in summer camps, Sunday School and with other groups of children. One thing was holding some of them back: finances. That burden could be lightened with help from this fund. So I talked with each one individually and learned that five of them needed help. They were definitely encouraged by this, and signed up for the next 2-week session of courses.

I could not even imagine the long-range effect this would have. One of our "boys" was studying law, but was not satisfied and wished he could do more to serve the Lord. As a result of the training and of working in a summer camp, he began looking into other branches of study involving children. He felt the Lord would have him work with handicapped children, so he abandoned law school and changed universities. He found these studies so satisfying that he smiled all the

CHAPTER 20: HIS HAND STILL GUIDES

time, and enjoyed working with chilldren so much that he took over as director of Awana Club.

Likewise one of our "girls" was preparing to work in a bank or with something financial. She, too, was unsatisfied, and after the training changed from her branch to study to become a teacher. Last year she was teaching fourth grade in the school right across the street from our apartment.

"Take Care Of Your Mother!"

Our four children had promised their dad they would take care of me as my symptoms worsened and age brought physical complications. They had always been so caring and considerate, calling me often, coming to help when needed, and giving advice on complicated matters. But even though I managed well by myself, the time would come when I would need someone close by

Our oldest daughter lived in the US; too far away. One of the directors at our mission office had encouraged us to remain in France because after more than 40 years on the field, it would be too difficult to adapt. This advice, plus the Lord's leading, convinced me to remain in France where I could continue to stay in touch with those unsaved friends and nedighbors.

Our second daughter is a doctor in northern France. The family has a large house which is not suitable for adding on a couiple of rooms for me.

My desire was to stay close to Argenteuil where I could continue at the church. Our son worked at Disneyland Paris on the other side of the "City of Lights" and lived in a studio, so there was definitely no room for me.

Our youngest daughter and her husband had three children by then, which made for a crowd in their small house. They were thinking of looking for something larger and farther away from the crowded suburbs. Our four children got together to discuss things, and agreed that it was most plausible for our youngest and her husband to find something large enough to renovate, allowing each of us to have private quarters. It should be close enough so we could help each other when needed, but yet give us enough independence to live our respective lives.

House-Hunting

So we set out on our quest to look for a large house that could be transformed, or one that had a small house on it's property. The first thing we learned was that everything in our combined price range needed so much work done that it would end up doubling the price. As we continued our search, Sebastien began looking into the price of buying a lot and having a house built, and found it was much more reasonable to build. He compared the quality

CHAPTER 20: HIS HAND STILL GUIDES

and price of different construction companies, and also searched for a lot zoned for construction.

Finally he decided on a lot in a small town of 1000 residents with a lovely castle, activities for the children, excellent schools, a music school and a park. My daughter and I were in agreement and signed the papers for the land and the house.

Why am I telling you all this? In France there is a definite problem concerning care for the elderly. Many times the children work full-time and have a busy life, therefore they look for a retirement home at a reasonable price and park their parents if they can afford it. Others allow their parents to live alone and try to get by to see them from time to time.

One summer a few years ago many people went on vacation and left their parents for up to a month to fend for themselves. That year in August, France had heat wave and literally thousands of the aged died of dehydration and sunstroke. Since that time, every summer there is a campaign to remind the population to check on their loved ones, their elderly friends and neighbors, to make sure that they drink enough, have a cool place to relax, and are loosely dressed.

Now when we share with others how the Lord answered prayer for adequate quarters for both an active family and a "mother-in-law", and especially

HIS HAND IN OUR LIVES

how we all live in relative harmony, it is a good testimony. Many people don't believe it can be done, and show their surprise, commenting that it is an ideal situation and that every family should take care of their elderly parents.

Our gracious Lord has answered so many prayer reqests that it is impossible to count them all. What is so wonderful is that, when we come to a time in our lives where everything and everybody seems to be against us, and we think the Lord doesn't even hear our cries, that is the time to remember all the many times God has answered and brought us through, triumphantly! He will do so again and again and again! We may not understand how, but He is faithful in all His ways.

Listen to what the Psalmist says:

"For this God,

Is our God for ever and ever:

He will be our guide

Even unto death."

(Psalm 48:14)

ABOUT THE AUTHOR

Born in Westfield, Massachusetts, Gail Blanchard Huffman began her life in cold country. Her parents acquired a dairy farm in Piermont, New Hampshire. A brother and a sister were born there.

At 8 years of age, she moved to Florida with her family because of her brother's health. That opened a whole new world!

Her primary schooling took place in Plant City, and Junior High in Tampa after a move to Temple Terrrace. From there she went to Hillsborough High School and graduated in 1961. While there, she was a member of Future Homemakers of America and the National Honor Society.

She received the Crisco Award for her activities in Future Homemakers.

For further education she began studies at Tennessee Temple University, Chattanooga, TN in

1961 and graduated with a Bachelor of Arts in 1968.

In 1962 she marrried Robert (Bob) Huffman, and together they answered the call of the Lord to serve Him in France as church-planting missionaries with Baptist International Missions, Inc. Language studies followed at the Alliance Francaise in Paris, France.

After settling in Argenteuil, France, a suburb of Paris, they established the Bible Baptist Church. They are parents of four children, two of whom were born in Chattanooga and two in France.

www.ingramcontent.com/pod-product-compliance
Lightning Source LLC
Chambersburg PA
CBHW071329190426
43193CB00041B/1032